Praise for *Brands Win Championships*

" *Brands Win Championships* is an easy and informative read. The theory of creating a strong brand stands true in my time with three of the programs I built. The University of Miami was going to cancel football before I arrived—today one of the country's top athletic brands, known as 'The U.'

"It took a strong marketing effort to create that brand and get the community behind us. Because of this effort, we were able to build a dynasty. The same is true with the University of Louisville when I arrived at that program as well as the creation of Florida Atlantic University's football program. We needed to create a brand where there was not one.

"*Brands Win Championships* takes you through some of the country's top stories and teaches you how to build a winning brand."

—**Howard Schnellenberger**, Head Football Coach, University of Miami, National Championship 1983

" *Brands Win Championships* is a must-read for anyone in sports marketing. We can talk about tradition all we want, but this book sees the future and shows you how to get there."

—**Nate Scott**, *USA Today Sports,* For the Win

" An excellent read. I would absolutely recommend this book to any coach or athletic director. Brands DO win!"

—**Anson Dorrance**, Women's Head Soccer Coach, University of North Carolina, 22-Time National Champion and 1991 World Championship Coach

" If you are in college sports marketing, then *Brands Win Championships* should definitely be a part of your strategic plan."

—**Chris Yandle**, Assistant Athletic Director, Georgia Tech University

" Jeremy Darlow is a gifted and talented digital marketing and brand expert. Jeremy's book *Brands Win Championships* provides the reader a playbook on how to create and manage your brand for optimal performance and results. "

—**Brent Jones**, Associate Athletic Director of Marketing and Communications, Southern Miss

" Jeremy Darlow's new book on branding, *Brands Win Championships*, is an essential read for the current athletic department practitioner and the rising sport management major. This book is a must-read for anyone looking to gain a place or solidify their place in the market. "

—**David Haase**, Assistant Athletic Director, University of West Georgia

" I love this book. A must-read for sports marketing classes and athletic departments, big or small. "

—**Darin W. White, PhD**, Chair, American Marketing Association Sports Marketing Academic Society; Professor of Marketing, Brock School of Business, Samford University

" Extremely thorough, entertaining, and thought-provoking. As a mid-major athletic department in an environment dominated by some FBS programs, we need all the help we can get to establish our unique brand in the sports market, and this book filled with useful information that we'll be able to employ. "

—**Craig Coleman**, Director of Athletics, Robert Morris University

" Great read! Entertaining and informative, a brand-building guide for programs of any size. "

—**Gary Clark**, Director of Athletics, Furman University

"Brand truly matters in college sports. Jeremy Darlow has laid out all the important aspects to effective branding. His approach will make a difference for all programs which embrace the concept."

—**Brad Teague, PhD**, Athletic Director, University of Central Arkansas

"*Brands Win Championships* stands as a must-read book for intercollegiate athletic administrators. With a laser focus on the college athletics model, Darlow delves deep into the kind of brand-building action that will lead to sustained success."

—**Russell Houghtaling**, Director of Digital Media, University of Oklahoma

"*Brands Win Championships* gives coaches and administrators a great playbook for what it takes in today's world to get your message and vision out to fans, alumni, boosters, and, most importantly, recruits."

—**Mike Gambino**, Head Baseball Coach, Boston College

"*Brands Win Championships* is a great asset to any intercollegiate athletic department looking to identify, create, and develop their brand. Jeremy has provided a valuable tool for any external relations staff in fundraising, sales, and/or marketing."

—**Tim Collins**, Assistant Athletic Director of Development, University of Wyoming

"I would recommend this book to every equipment manager out there. This is a must-read."

—**Augustine Hernandez**, Assistant Athletic Director for Equipment Services, Eastern Washington University

brands

~~**defenses**~~ **win**

championships

brands
~~defenses~~ win
championships

the secret to winning a national title in the 21st century

by Jeremy Darlow

jack + june
publishing

Jack and June Publishing, Portland, OR 97209

Editing by Vinnie Kinsella and Kristen Hall-Geisler

Cover image by Mako Miyamoto

Book design by Ceci Sorochin

ISBN: 978-0-9905622-0-7

dedicated to

Jack & June

Darlow

forever my inspiration

1

managing
your perception

2

writing
your story

3

telling
your story

conclusion

intro

The University of Oregon will win more games in the next ten years than any other school in college football, and there isn't a single program in America equipped to stop them...yet.

You might be surprised to hear that the reason for this impending success has less to do with coaching and has more to do with marketing. In ten years the University of Oregon will be the premier program in college football because its marketing department is building a brand in Eugene, Oregon, whereas other schools are building teams in four-year, unsustainable increments. The days of your parents' college athletics are over. Dead. Gone. Not. Coming. Back. It's not just about x's and o's anymore; it's also about polarizing uniforms and massive billboards in Times Square. The University of Oregon football program is a Mac, and everyone else is a PC.

So, how did we get here? How can Oregon be more relevant, more powerful, more prestigious than LSU, USC, and Texas? How can that be? Believe it or not, it's not about the money as much as it is about the strategy. The University of Oregon has some of the brightest marketing minds in the world building a freight train of a brand that has taken college athletics (not just football) by storm. No one saw this coming, and no one seems to have figured out a way to stop it. The reason? People are still trying to solve the Oregon Duck offense instead of looking at how that offense came to be so explosive: branding.

I'll say it again: it's not just about the x's and o's anymore. It's about the brand. But the intent of this book is not simply to point out the demise of every college athletic program in the country not named the University of Oregon. It's quite the opposite. As a matter of fact, being a proud graduate of Oregon State University, the Ducks' own in-state rival, I would love nothing more than to help thwart such things from happening, by equipping you with the tools necessary to build your own brands.

As the head of brand and digital marketing for football and baseball at adidas, I've been fortunate to work with some of the strongest brand names in college athletics, including the University of Notre Dame, the University of Michigan, and the University of California, Los Angeles, to name a few. Collaborating with some of the brightest and most passionate people in the industry, I've been responsible for brand strategy and content development for a wide range of schools. Working with everyone from traditional powers to upstarts looking to make names for themselves, and activating at everything from the College World Series (CWS) to the BCS National Championship, it's been my job to elevate each of our schools to a level that differentiates it from the competition and attracts the best high school athletes in the country.

In ten years the most powerful person at an athletic program will no longer be the head coach; instead, the most powerful person will be the individual in charge of managing and building the brand. This book is meant to act as your roadmap to successfully developing your brand and elevating your program to levels it has never seen.

brands win championships—and i'm going to show you how.

1

managing
your perception

making old men angry, and why I love my job

My dream job in college was to run brand marketing for one of the country's major football brands. Being from Portland, Oregon, I was looking at either adidas or Nike, both of which are headquartered locally. After returning home from a four-year stint in San Francisco in 2009, I was lucky enough to get that chance with adidas. By that time I had been blessed with the opportunity to be part of some of the most successful brand launches and campaigns in two other major industries: video games and beer. No, you didn't read that wrong. I went from video games to beer to football; what more can a guy ask for, right?

Shortly after I started at adidas, I was tasked with launching what we call strategy uniforms for some of the brand's most prestigious NCAA football properties. Strategy uniforms are unique uniform designs that, in many cases, are worn only once in a season and are usually reserved for big games. One of those first uniform designs was unlike anything anyone had ever seen or would have expected from a school with, in this case, incredible history and tradition. The school was Notre Dame, and the uniform was sure to cause a stir.

So, there I was, still fairly new to the job, brand-new to the category, and one of my first projects was to launch a uniform that was no doubt going to spark a firestorm of criticism among the staunch, traditionalist Notre Dame alumni. I needed a plan.

Having passionately followed college athletics as a fan for years, and after digging into the situation and the school, I knew we were dealing with two very different communities. One was the high school kids, who at this point had seen several new uniforms from schools all over the country with varying degrees of boldness. And for the most part, these kids loved them. I wasn't worried about the high school community. Then we had essentially the antithesis of these kids: the older, mostly male alumni who were steeped in the school's glorious past and tradition and were generally adverse to change. Despite the disparity in digital aptitude between the two groups, it is this group, the older postgraduate fans, whose voices ring louder online when it comes to their school's athletic programs—especially when they're not happy. I knew our perceived success at launch would hinge on winning over this crowd—the question was how.

brands <mark>defenses</mark> win championships

Between our brand team at adidas and the university's athletic department, we needed to create the perception that this new uniform was loved *before* the alumni even had a chance to judge for themselves. Delivering an opinion, rather than playing the waiting game and leaving the uniform open for criticism, was a much safer bet. We knew we had something on our side: recruiting. College sports are all about recruiting, and the reason every school launches a special uniform (or two) these days is because high school kids love them. We also knew that if the players loved them, the fans had no choice but to fall in line.

We built our launch plan around this idea. Together with the school, we focused initial launch assets around premium photo and video content, complemented by reactions from the team's two captains, all of which were shared with the national and local media. The alum who has followed the program since he was a boy and hates change would not only see our photos and video but also see video reaction from his favorite players, excited over what they considered a "sweet" uniform. We made sure that at launch our communication around the new design was accompanied by athlete feedback, which happened to be very positive.

If we were to launch the uniform without any explanation or player support, simply releasing imagery to the media and letting this older, more steadfast group judge the uniform for themselves, we would have no doubt been flooded with negative comments. The overall consensus would have been that adidas failed in its design. Instead we were able to preempt opinions because, as many of the online responses from fans read, "If the players like it, I like it. It's all about recruiting." For our purpose, it was all about perception.

Perception plays a role in everything we do in brand marketing, especially when it comes to marketing NCAA programs. A quick refresher on the role perception plays in college athletics can take your communication strategies and athletic program from bad to good or good to great.

teens pick brands;
pros pick contracts

Perception is what college athletic departments across the country are built on. It's the foundation. What people think about a university or athletic program dictates success, and that's because, unlike in professional sports, the rich get richer in college athletics.

Teams with the worst record one year don't have the luxury of acquiring the number one draft choice in the next. Blue-chip high school athletes hold all the cards, and they're choosing between brands. As a result, schools like Notre Dame, Ohio State, and USC reel in the nation's top football players year after year, while schools like Duke, Louisville, and Kentucky routinely garner commitments from the nation's basketball elite. The same holds true for every sport in college athletics: certain programs, by consistently winning, have built enormous equity in their brand.

> **blue-chip high school athletes hold all the cards, and they're choosing between brands.**

There are a lot of definitions of *brand equity* on the internet these days. In simple terms brand equity is the combination of strength and awareness. Strength in terms of *what* people think about your brand and awareness meaning *how much* they think about your brand. Essentially, do they know you, and do they like you? Brand equity, for the most part, is based on perception.

The aforementioned programs have established a perception of athletic pedigree and tradition that, regardless of a down season here or there, keeps them competing for the country's best talent each year.

brand equity is the combination of strength and awareness.

your reputation precedes you

What if your school doesn't have a storied tradition of winning? How can you get your program to that level? On the flip side, if you are UCLA, how do you take an already successful baseball program and make it stronger?

It starts by building and increasing perception that your school, in fact, does belong at the level you are striving to reach. Building perception is the beginning of a domino effect that can and will improve your program, no matter what situation it finds itself in.

 Ask yourself the following:

➧ **How can a program take a breakout season and turn it into long-term success?**
➧ **How can an already solid program become one of the nation's elite?**
➧ **How can a perennial doormat move up in the standings?**
➧ **How can a traditional power increase its reach (to new fans, recruits, etc.) even further?**

The answers to these questions can be found on the following pages, and they all originate from the same place: perception. Each of the lessons outlined in this book in one way or another has to do with building and influencing perception—yes, it's that important.

Take, for example, the ongoing struggle smaller conference teams face when it comes to athletics. Smaller conferences have a harder time competing with the (former) Bowl Championship Series (BCS) conferences because, in the eyes of mainstream America, those three letters stood for *Big-Time College Sports*. As a result every other conference is perceived as second-rate. The *Daily Aztec*, San Diego State's independent student paper, once wrote in a story regarding the effect of perception on the Mountain West Conference: "Perception is reality in college athletics. It matters not that the top football and men's basketball teams in the Mountain West Conference are as competitive, and in some cases as talented, as in the [former] Pac-10 conference. Nor do the equivalents in coaching and academic standards matter to fans" (August 20, 2007). This statement may have been a bit skewed by the writer's affiliations, but it's hard to argue against the idea that a top-five team from a (former) BCS or College Football Playoff (CFP) conference is looked at and perceived differently from a top-five team from a non-CFP conference.

who you calling david, goliath?

Before the 2007 Fiesta Bowl between Boise State and Oklahoma, who'd you think was going to win, truthfully? There aren't many people out there who would have picked Boise State, despite the fact that they were ranked #9, only two spots behind #7 Oklahoma. The reason? Oklahoma is in the Big 12 and has a storied history, while Boise State played in the Western Athletic Conference on blue turf. The Broncos were seen as a gimmick, nothing more. That perception remained intact after the game, despite Boise State's landmark victory over the Sooners.

Perception doesn't win games, but it does win recruiting battles. The following year, Oklahoma didn't lose to Boise State in the recruiting war, despite the Broncos' victory on the field. It's hard to break free of people's perception of you; it takes time and a lot of effort. In the five years after the Broncos beat the Sooners, Boise State's recruiting rankings (according to Rivals.com) were as follows: 2007: #68; 2008: #89; 2009: #72; 2010: #82; 2011: #53. In those same seasons, the Broncos finished, ranked in the top fifteen four times, with one top-five and two top-ten finishes.

Winning is important to your long-term success as a program, but it's not enough to just win. You need to win *and* be sexy while you're doing it. You need to build a brand that kids want to be a part of. Those kids are your potential recruits. What makes a kid want to wear your badge?

you need to win *and* be sexy while you're doing it.

build your brand before you build a new stadium

Below is the first of two charts that will go a long way in providing you with a roadmap to building a successful program, and—surprise!—perception is the key to each. You're going to want to refer back to these throughout the book as you begin to formulate plans of your own. Speaking of which, I have included notes pages after each chapter for you to write down the beginnings of a winning communication strategy. When ideas pop into your head—and they will—write them down!

The following is a visual representation of what I call the Athletic Program Life Cycle.

The Athletic Program Life Cycle has four stages: perception, recruiting, winning, and money. What is clear is that each of the pieces is extremely important and yet dependent on one another. Before we move on, ask yourself the following:

➧ Can a program successfully recruit when people have the perception of it being a doormat or that of a weaker program?
Not likely.

➧ Can a program win a national championship with poor recruiting classes?
If the program is lucky enough to land an incredible coach, maybe; but again, it's not likely.

➧ Can a program expect boosters to pour money into a consistently losing program?
The cycle usually goes: win and the dollars will follow, not the other way around.

If you are not a traditional athletic power, the future would seem dire, according to the answers to these questions; however, that is where the power of perception comes in!

Take a look back at the life cycle. Which of those four stages do you think is the most easily influenced? If you said perception, I would absolutely agree with you. Let's break down each stage in the life cycle, starting with recruiting. Imagine for a moment that you are an athletic director trying to turn around a losing program or increase the reach of a successful program. Let's dissect what kind of impact you can have on each of the building blocks as you try to increase the stature and success of your team.

recruiting. Unfortunately, recruiting success is not elastic. In most cases if a program is not winning, it takes a coaching change or a major investment in facilities to turn around underperforming recruiting efforts. One successful year usually does not lead to a major upswing in recruiting. The same can be said for already strong programs looking to reach elite status. It takes years of success to create relationships and recruiting pipelines.

Difficulty to Affect: Hard

winning. If you can't recruit to the level of your competition, chances are you can't consistently win against that competition. It becomes a brutal cycle that is very hard to break.

Difficulty to Affect: Hard

money. In most cases if a program is not winning, boosters will not be lining up at the athletic director's door to throw money at it. The further away from the top your program is in the standings, the further you push away potential boosters.

Difficulty to Affect: Hard

perception. The beautiful thing about perception is that it is elastic. It can be affected at any moment, no matter the situation. It is also the first domino to fall when attempting to increase the success of a program. By changing perception through a strategic, tactical story (I'll show you how to build a story in step 2), you can immediately improve your chances of recruiting and winning, as well as the amount of money brought in by boosters.

Difficulty to Affect: Easy

So the cycle begins. Perception dictates the level of talent considering playing for a school; better recruits provide an improved chance of winning; successful programs garner more money from boosters; money leads to the top-rate facilities that ultimately feed back through to the perception of a big-time program. Full circle. Bottom line: Start with perception. Of the four stages, perception is the most dynamic and the most malleable.

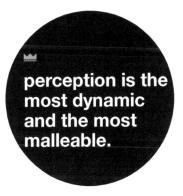

perception is the most dynamic and the most malleable.

don't build a rocket ship when you just need a camry

The Perception Scale represents how fans and media perceive a program (see Prestige, page 23) and consequently what type of media strategy should be employed (see Media, page 26).

It's important to realize all programs in the twenty-first century are *not* created equal; thus, neither are the communication strategies each should employ. Depending on the sport, the juggernauts of college athletics can and should take their stories and go about their communication efforts in a completely different way than smaller programs should. The Perception Scale acts as a communication strategy roadmap. There are four categories called out on the scale: prestige, reach, media, and cost. An explanation of each follows. Also note that the following school examples are based on my own opinion of each university's football program.

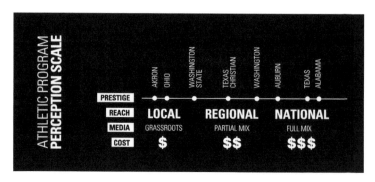

prestige

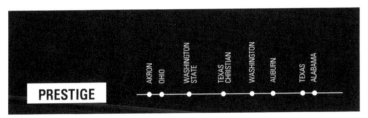

PRESTIGE

AKRON | OHIO | WASHINGTON STATE | TEXAS CHRISTIAN | WASHINGTON | AUBURN | TEXAS | ALABAMA

The prestige rating measures how a program is perceived nationally by fans and media alike. The further to the right a program sits on the scale, the more prestigious the program is (e.g., Notre Dame in football and Duke in basketball would both be on the right). Before using this scale, determine how your program is perceived today.

Be realistic when judging your program's prestige. If you self-inflate your program's reach, you will find yourself spending more money with little to show in return. If you're unsure, it's better to be conservative and adjust up as you go, so as to not waste money.

reach

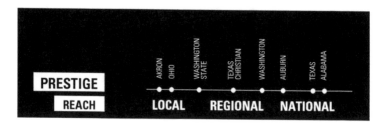

Reach outlines the level at which a program should be communicating. The less prestigious the program, the more geographically targeted the outreach strategy should be. On the flip side, if you have a strong reputation and tradition of success, like the University of Nebraska, which also happens to be the only major athletic program in the state, it makes more sense for you to take your communications beyond the state lines.

Knowing what route to take will depend entirely on your understanding of your school's reputation and perceived strength locally, regionally, and in a few cases nationally. If at any moment you're unsure of where your program stands, simply sit down at your computer and read. Among social media, message boards, and the major sporting news sites (ESPN.com, Yahoo Sports, etc.), you will quickly get a clear picture of how your school is viewed.

Let's take a look at the different levels of reach.

local. Before a program can start communicating on a grander
scale, it must ensure it has the support of its hometown and state. While all schools should be focusing attention on local communication and winning over the hometown audience, for some of the less prestigious, smaller schools, local communication becomes everything. As a school in

this situation finds success and starts to garner pickup in the media, thus expanding its overall awareness, it can then start looking at broadening its reach.

regional. If you are Texas Christian University, a regional strategy would include states where you have the most reach, such as: Texas, Oklahoma, Arizona, and Louisiana. It is also important to consider which of the major recruiting and media hotbed states you are closest to and include those areas in your campaign (Florida, California, and Texas in football, for example).

national. This is reserved for the major players in each sport (Alabama in football, North Carolina in basketball, Oregon State in baseball, etc.) who have built enough equity in their names to speak to a national audience effectively. All fifty states are available to you; pick and choose as you see fit.

media

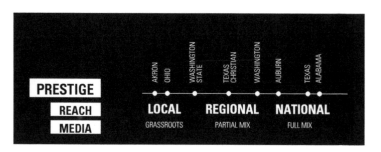

Media strategy depends solely on how a program is perceived, not on how much money it has to spend.

I've laid out the type of communication a program should be considering, depending on where it finds itself on the scale, while outlining three high-level media approaches to tactically marketing your program. Each approach is differentiated by level of investment as well as reach.

grassroots marketing consists of nontraditional, budget-conscious methods to get your message across—things like social media, brand ambassadors, or street teams and wild postings (the 11″ x 17″-sized posters you'll find lining walls and windows in major cities, usually touting an album release or new movie).

partial media mix consists of local grassroots marketing efforts as well as some traditional media vehicles like TV, print, digital, radio, out of home, and direct mail.

full media mix consists of local grassroots marketing efforts along with all of the traditional media vehicles.

The further a program is to the right of the Perception Scale, the more money and creativity it will take to make an impact. The reason is twofold. One, fans, media, and recruits are much more careful about the programs they anoint to elite status, meaning each level of perception becomes harder and harder to penetrate. Two, if a program is successful, chances are those same fans, media, and recruits are already used to hearing about it through the media and the people around them. Because of this white noise born from the program's success, any additional attention given to the program may get lost in the shuffle. As a result it becomes much harder to make an impression. If you find your program in this situation, the key to your communication strategy becomes disruption, meaning anything you do must look, feel, and sound different from the typical approach of other programs in your sport category. Along with the need to be unique in *what* you communicate comes the need to be unique in *how* you communicate. In order to break through this white noise you've built through consistent winning and adoration from the media and fans, you need to be bold, brave, and loud in how you communicate. What can you do to turn heads and get people talking about your program?

On the opposite side of the scale, a perennially bottom-feeding program will have a much easier time making an impact for these same reasons, just reversed. One, people are slow to crown a king but quick to identify a Cinderella. (Everyone loves a good Cinderella story; see the aforementioned Boise State football or Butler basketball.) Two, little success brings little media attention, which means any communication a traditionally unsuccessful program is able to engineer becomes unexpected and quickly breaks through the clutter.

If you find your program in between strategies, continue to execute tactics found to the left of the scale while selectively taking ideas from the next strategy up. For instance, if your program is in between the grassroots and partial media mix strategies based on program prestige, continue full steam ahead with grassroots efforts while strategically choosing pieces of traditional media that make sense for your program, audience, and budget.

The thing to remember about strategy is that no matter how far to the right of the scale your program goes, always keep one eye on the rearview mirror (or in this case, anything left of your position on the scale) and continue to do the little things that got you there. This means that if your program is lucky enough to have reached elite-level status, you will need to not only employ more tactics from the full media mix but also continue to activate at the grassroots level. Marketing professionals call this "Goliath acting like David."

cost

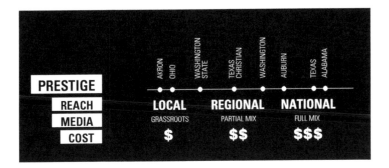

Cost of entry signifies how much a marketing campaign would cost relatively, depending on where a program finds itself on the Perception Scale. As programs move to the right of the scale and the media mix becomes more substantial, the cost of the campaign naturally becomes more expensive.

The best brand marketers in the world embrace the power of perception and use it to their advantage. Now it's your turn. In step 2, we're going to take what we've learned about perception and turn it into a differentiating brand story for your program.

CH1 MANAGING YOUR PERCEPTION

COLLEGE ATHLETICS
LIFE CYCLE

PERCEPTION

RECRUITING

$$$
MONEY

WINNING

PERCEPTION DRIVES
RECRUITING
BECAUSE...

TEENS PICK **BRANDS**, PROS PICK **CONTRACTS**

 IT TAKES MORE THAN WINS
TO BUILD A BRAND THAT ATTRACTS RECRUITS

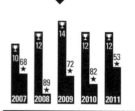

BOISE STATE WINS **VS** RECRUITING RANKING

WINS
R.RANK

73RD
BOISE STATE
FOOTBALL'S AVERAGE RECRUITING
CLASS RANKING FROM 2007 TO 2011
ACCORDING TO RIVALS.COM

BRAND PERCEPTION LEADS TO RECRUITING SUCCESS. RECRUITING SUCCESS LEADS TO

► CHAMPIONSHIPS ◄

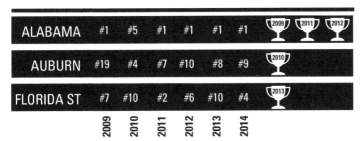

	2009	2010	2011	2012	2013	2014	
ALABAMA	#1	#5	#1	#1	#1	#1	🏆2009 🏆2011 🏆2012
AUBURN	#19	#4	#7	#10	#8	#9	🏆2010
FLORIDA ST	#7	#10	#2	#6	#10	#4	🏆2013

RECRUITING CLASS RANKING OF THE THREE NATIONAL CHAMPIONSHIP WINNING FOOTBALL PROGRAMS FROM 2009 TO 2014 ACCORDING TO RIVALS.COM

■■■■ CHAMPIONSHIPS LEAD TO MORE MONEY ■■■■

$89M

THE AMOUT OF REVENUE GENERATED BY THE ALABAMA FOOTBALL PROGRAM IN 2013, A 16% INCREASE SINCE ITS 2011 NATIONAL TITLE, ACCORDING TO FORBES.COM

YOUR PROGRAM IS A BRAND. YOU ARE A BRAND MANAGER.

START THINKING THAT WAY.

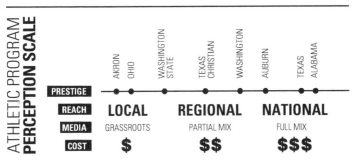

ATHLETIC PROGRAM PERCEPTION SCALE

	AKRON / OHIO	WASHINGTON STATE	TEXAS CHRISTIAN	WASHINGTON	AUBURN	TEXAS / ALABAMA

PRESTIGE
REACH — LOCAL — REGIONAL — NATIONAL
MEDIA — GRASSROOTS — PARTIAL MIX — FULL MIX
COST — $ — $$ — $$$

CH1 HOMEWORK

⇒ How would your program rate (1–10) based on each of the four stages that make up the Athletic Program Life Cycle? Which areas need the most attention?

perception 1 2 3 4 5 6 7 8 9 10
recruiting 1 2 3 4 5 6 7 8 9 10
winning 1 2 3 4 5 6 7 8 9 10
money/facilities 1 2 3 4 5 6 7 8 9 10

....

⇒ How is your program perceived by local, regional, and national audiences? What do they say about you?

◆ Where does your program sit on the Perception Scale? What does that mean for the type of communication strategy you need to employ?

YOUR ATHLETIC PROGRAM **PERCEPTION SCALE**

PRESTIGE
REACH
MEDIA
COST

LOCAL
GRASSROOTS
$

REGIONAL
PARTIAL MIX
$$

NATIONAL
FULL MIX
$$$

notes

....

2
writing
your story

strong brands start with great stories

All right, you get it. Perception is crucial. Now let's start using it to your advantage. The second step to building a winning athletic program through marketing is to write a brand story. Don't get scared by the word *brand* or try to overcomplicate things. A brand story is just as it sounds—a story, albeit a *true* story, and your program is a brand. From here on out, consider yourself a brand manager and a storyteller with the goal of sharing what you know to be good—no, *great*—and exciting about your program with the rest of the world.

consider yourself
a brand manager
and a storyteller.

To put you in the right frame of mind, here are some of my favorite brand stories written in recent years:

pcs are for nerds

Apple has written a story about a computer that not only has everything you need in a laptop but also makes you feel young, hip, and cool. Many will buy Macs based solely on the brand's story and the way owning a Mac makes them feel, not on the computer's functionality.

cigarettes are for men

Marlboro wrote an effective brand story in the 1950s that read like a script from a John Wayne movie. The company's story was about a cigarette made for the American cowboy, a real man's man. If you considered yourself a man's man and liked to smoke, chances are Marlboro was your cigarette of choice.

"i am the greatest"

Individual athletes have brand stories too. Muhammad Ali was one of the first, if not the first, to write his own brand story. In Ali's case the story was about being the greatest in all things. He was the greatest boxer, the greatest athlete, the greatest sports icon, the greatest trash-talker, and ultimately the greatest self-promoter. Regardless of where he truly ranks among the best boxers in history, the man who floated like a butterfly and stung like a bee will always be considered one of the greatest because that's the story he told.

Let's look at a couple brand stories from a pair of collegiate sports programs of today:

football, uniforms, and a fancy weight room.
The University of Oregon's story is about being the college football program of the future, driven by a fast, exciting offense, state-of-the-art facilities, and outlandish, attention-grabbing uniforms. By telling stories seventeen- and eighteen-year-old kids can relate to, the Ducks have made major inroads with blue-chip athletes outside of the Northwest.

basketball, polos, and the legendary coach k.
The Duke Blue Devils' story is about excellence on and off the basketball court. Driving that message is a sophisticated, polished, and not to mention legendary head coach—Mike Krzyzewski. Today, when you think of Duke, you think of basketball brilliance, but you also think of a group of respectful, well-mannered young men whom you wouldn't mind your daughter bringing home.

people are talking behind your back

Jeff Bezos, founder, CEO, and chairman of the board of Amazon, is often credited with best describing what a brand is: "It's what people say about you when you're not in the room." I don't know about you, but that sounds an awful lot like perception to me. By writing a brand story, you will begin to change perceptions about your program and ultimately affect what fans, media, and recruits are saying about you when you're not there. But how?

It starts with differentiation. In the world of branding (and recruiting), differentiation is key. There are hundreds of programs promoting the same reasons to attend their universities (location, playing time, facilities, etc.); a relevant and compelling brand story can break through that noise and differentiate your program.

92%
92 percent of people trust recommendations from friends or family above all other forms of advertising when making a purchase decision.

Once you have a unique position among your competition, you'll start to drive word of mouth. *Business News Daily* reported that 92 percent of people trust recommendations from friends or family above all other forms of advertising when making a purchase decision (April 13, 2012). Bottom

JEREMY DARLOW

line: word of mouth is more effective when it comes to swaying opinions. If you write a story people believe in and are excited about, they will tell their friends, and your legend will grow. There are thousands of sports fans in America without allegiance to any particular program. They are up for grabs! By telling a story that people can relate to, you will begin to see fans with no previous ties to your university rooting for your program. Depending on where they live and how good of a story you tell, these newfound fans will ultimately begin to fill your stadium as well.

From those conversations, especially those taking place in the social stratosphere, the media will no doubt catch wind. Reporters love a good story; it's the foundation of their work. Give them a pertinent story, and watch them build your program's awareness for you. I don't know how many times I heard the legend of Alexis Serna, the former Oregon State University kicker who missed three extra points against LSU in his first game (one the Beavers ultimately lost in overtime) only to come back and win the Lou Groza Award as the nation's top kicker in his sophomore season. The media eat stories like this up, and many times these tales become national in reach, which in turn grows the number of eyes on your program. Help the media help you.

Media support brings awareness to your story and helps that story withstand the test of time. A story that people believe in runs deeper than wins or losses. An authentic and meaningful story will have people rooting not only for your program but also for what your program stands for. Win or lose, that's a much harder bond to break.

Finally, at the end of the day, it is about winning. The

> ◢
> **an authentic and meaningful story will have people rooting not only for your program but also for what your program stands for.**

combination of being extraordinary, driving buzz, leveraging the media, and building an army of ambassadors (all of which we'll cover on the forthcoming pages) will only help you recruit the best and the brightest high school athletes to your program. Recruiting better athletes off the field leads to success on it.

Write a compelling and genuine story, and you will begin to change your program's perception and fortunes.

grab a shovel and start digging

Okay, okay, you get the point. Writing a story is key to your success, but how do you do it?

The first step in creating a brand story is to do what marketing aficionado Scott Bedbury calls a "big dig," a technique he employed as he helped build coffee giant Starbucks into a successful brand. In his book *A New Brand World*, Bedbury recounted challenging his team to "dig deeply into everything that [had] been written, felt, said, or thought about coffee" (2002). Do the same in your space.

Grab your shovel and let's dig.

go undercover

Start with your audience. In order to truly understand what makes the fans and media who follow your sport and program tick, you need to do research—a lot of research. Sit in the heart of your student section during a game; go to a sports bar during another. Spend half of one game sitting with boosters and the other half with the media. Spend an entire game monitoring your team's message boards and social spaces. To truly make a positive impact on your audience, you need to see what they see, hear what they hear, and feel what they feel. Once you can think like them and empathize with them, you can tell a story to them.

> to truly make a positive impact on your audience, you need to see what they see, hear what they hear, and feel what they feel.

look in the mirror

Once you understand your audience better, it's time to get to know your program. Go through everything you can find about your program through present day, including old statistics, former and current player rosters and bios, coaching bios, written articles, media guides, and team monikers. Your objective is to discover and reveal the essence of your program. What makes it special? What is it about your program that keeps fans coming back?

In some cases a journalist following your program will have put that essence into words in a previously written article. In other cases the idea will be completely buried in the hallowed halls of your stadium or arena. Find your program's essence and let it free.

Here are a few places to start looking:

crosstown rivals. Looking at what, in many cases, is your program's antithesis can make its essence more apparent (i.e., your program may be your rival's exact opposite).

former coaches and players. Many programs have had a revered coach or player at some point in their histories, and in many cases it is what these individuals stood for and how they presented themselves that is remembered most. Think about former football coach Bear Bryant at Alabama, former basketball coach John Wooden at UCLA, and former wrestling coach Dale Thomas at Oregon State. Similarly consider former soccer player Mia Hamm at North Carolina, former baseball player Reggie Jackson at Arizona State, and former football player Peyton Manning at the University of Tennessee. Your program's essence may lie in the character of someone who once walked your halls.

location. Your program's essence may be in your own back-yard. What makes your city, town, or community unique may be what makes your program unique.

traditions. College sports are about tradition, and there is a good chance your program has a tradition or two. Do a separate dig into the core of those traditions, and you may find the essence you're looking for.

the cleveland lebrons

One mistake I see many professional sports teams consistently make is building their stories around a current player or players. Consider what happened in Cleveland when LeBron James decided to take his talents to South Beach. Putting all the eggs in an individual player's basket did not bode well for Cleveland. According to a *Huffington Post* article, the Cleveland Cavaliers went from having the second best attendance numbers in the NBA, during LeBron's last season, to having the nineteenth best attendance numbers just two years later (June 2012).

Don't fall victim to this gaffe. Focusing on current players who will not be around in four years does nothing to build loyalty and long-term identity for your program. The LeBron Jameses of the world should absolutely be a part of a campaign, but players should be reinforcing your story rather than being your story.

2nd

the cleveland cavaliers went from having the second best attendance numbers in the nba, during lebron's last season, to having the nineteenth best attendance numbers just two years later.

19th

put pen to paper

Once you've discovered your program's essence, you are ready to write your story. Make it short, make it simple, make it relevant, and make it memorable. Your brand story should be no more than a sentence long and should communicate in an understandable and concise manner what makes your program special. Remember the examples (my words, not theirs) used earlier:

OREGON
FOOTBALL
THE COLLEGE FOOTBALL PROGRAM OF THE FUTURE

DUKE
BASKETBALL
THE COLLEGE BASKETBALL PROGRAM DRIVEN BY EXCELLENCE ON AND OFF THE COURT

The story you write will not only drive your marketing communications, it will act as the internal mantra for your program. Every person in your athletic department, from the coaches to the team's part-time assistant, must live by your brand story or it will not succeed. Your story will be as successful as you make it.

Break your story and your program down to the DNA level, dissecting target, frame of reference, position, reasons to believe your story, and brand values. I've created my own example for Duke basketball for you to review and use as a guide:

duke basketball

→ Target

Twelve-to-eighteen-year-old basketball players, parents of prospective student athletes, national and local media covering basketball, and fans (current and potential)

→ Frame of Reference

Duke is the college basketball program…

→ Story

…built by excellence on and off the court.

→ Reasons to Believe:

Duke is one of the most successful college basketball programs of all time.

Duke consistently turns over talented alumni to the National Basketball Association.

Duke is considered one of the top educational institutions in the country.

Duke graduates its players at a consistently high level.

→ Values

Integrity, honor, excellence, class, sportsmanship, leadership

If you don't already have a brand manager in your marketing department, get one—fast. It should be clear now that your program and university are indeed brands and should be managed as such. In the twenty-first century, strategic marketing and brand management will be essential to building long-term and successful programs. It will be this person's job to ensure your brand story is being lived out by those within the university and is being told consistently and effectively at all levels of communication.

Before you begin writing, there are a few key rules or philosophies to remember when developing your story.

in the twenty-first century, strategic marketing and brand management will be essential to building long-term and successful programs.

don't be a liar

Stop lying. If you try building a story that is not genuine, it will fail, plain and simple. We live in what Seth Godin (another great marketing mind) called in his book *All Marketers Are Liars* (2004) a "low-trust world," meaning people will always look at a marketing campaign with a skeptical eye. People don't trust marketing. We need to see it to believe it. The second someone finds a crack in your brand story's armor, you've lost that person (potentially the people in their circle as well). If your story is not authentic and isn't being carried out every day and on every level by your program, it will show, and you will fail. Worse, you will have lost the faith of your fans, setting your program back years.

keep it stupid simple

We're a simple species, let's be honest. And it's the least complicated ideas that tend to stick. The goal of any successful communication platform is to create a simple message. It doesn't matter if you have the greatest, most compelling brand story anyone has ever come across—if no one knows what it means, it won't be effective.

you have eight seconds

When I say *story*, I don't mean you have to write a novel. Your message to parents, fans, recruits, media, whomever it is, has to be quick and to the point. Research suggests you have at most eight seconds to capture the attention of the audience you are speaking to, which, according to data site Statistic Brain, is the attention span of the average person as of 2013. One second less than that of a goldfish and four seconds less than the average human attention span back in 2000. We as a society do not have the patience to decipher a message. When I'm judging creative, my rule is that people need to "get it" in three to five seconds; that is how simple the story has to be. If it takes work from our brains, we move on. It sounds obvious, it sounds narrow-minded, but it's very important.

8"

eight seconds is the attention span of the average person as of 2013.

If you don't believe me, think about yourself for a moment. Do you pay attention to every ad on television? Do you scrutinize every print or web advertisement to fully understand what it is the brand is trying to communicate? I didn't think so. Now, people may be a little more open to listening to a message from your program because they have a genuine interest in sports or they are invested in your university, but they're still only going to give you a few seconds to capture their attention. Your brand story needs to be simple, and to the point.

remind me of your name again?

For years I've struggled to remember people's names. Knowing how important a name is to building relationships and how important relationships are in life and to me personally, I took to the Google machine to figure out how to improve. I came across a really interesting article, written by Jacquelyn Smith, titled, "6 Easy Ways to Remember Someone's Name" (*Forbes*, 2013). The article included tips to help you remember a person's name in that initial moment of interaction. One of the keys was repetition. The article suggested that after making a new acquaintance, the person should immediately say the name aloud at least twice. According to Darlene Price, author of *Well Said!: Presentations and Conversations That Get Results:* "Repetition engraves the person's name into your memory" (2012).

Marketing is no different. Our brains work in the same ways, no matter the situation. The more times people are exposed to your story, the more likely they are to understand and remember it. Everything you do as a program should derive from your brand story, with the repetition of

the more times people are exposed to your story, the more likely they are to understand and remember it.

that story being the glue that makes it stick. Just as Scott Bedbury alluded to in *A New Brand World*, whether it's the music people listen to while on hold to buy season tickets or the way in which the gameday program is designed, everything must be aligned with and speak to your story. In a society of busy people with little time to stop and listen, it is extremely important to utilize repetition in your tactics. A 2012 Facebook study showed that if brands reallocated media dollars to ensuring higher frequency of their ads, those brands could see a 40 percent increase in ROI with the same budget.

and i care because?

If your audience can't relate to your story, it won't matter how simple, quick, or genuine it is. If you are going to strike a chord, your story must be relevant. Duke basketball's brand story, for instance, is built on class, excellence, and integrity on and off the court. The Duke story is relevant because its audience presumes to carry themselves in the same manner. Duke is an educational institution built on these values, and many of those who attended and follow the university can relate to them.

who wants to know?

There are four main targets all college athletic programs must consider when developing communication strategies: fans, parents, recruits, and media. Each comes with its own set of motivations and requires unique communication strategies and forms of engagement. Just as a global company cannot expect a homogenous campaign to resonate with all cultures around the world, an NCAA brand cannot treat recruits the same way it treats parents. While the story should remain consistent, the way in which it's delivered must allow for versatility, dependent on the audience. Let's break down the differences and tendencies of each group.

"i can't believe we lost. season's over." —die-hard fan

We can spend days dissecting each category of fan based on loyalty alone, but for our purposes I've broken it down to three main segments: die-hard fans, casual fans, and potential fans. Fans are the soldiers on your front line; they will be only as effective in promoting your program as you are effective in leading it.

Die-hard fans are the most extreme of the three groups. This set takes the word *fan* to the next level. They're not called die-hard for nothing, as each seemingly lives and dies by your program's success. Usually well versed in the sport at hand, the die-hard fan is your biggest advocate and your harshest critic. This group knows your sport inside and out, and they know your program better than some in your athletic department. These folks are easy to identify, especially on the road. The die-hard fan proudly waves four flags, one from each window of his or her school-colored car, which has limited visibility in the rear thanks to the oversized school logo decal on the back window.

Die-hard fans want your program to succeed so bad it hurts. Because of that, many are more than willing to help you communicate your program's story, but you need to ask for their help and guide them. Companies all over the country are hiring street teams to promote their brands for an outrageous amount of money. I am willing to bet that you already have a group of ambassadors eager to do the same job for you—except they'll work for free. And because this group already knows a great deal about your program and believes in it, they'll do it better.

Feed the animals, as I like to say. Involve your hardcore fan base in your communication strategy. They will scream your story from the highest hills in your town if you ask them to. I cannot overstate the importance of this group. Win their hearts, and they will steal many more from your competitors.

It is from this group that you will begin to build an army of ambassadors. Do whatever you have to do to ignite the fire within and bring them in to help you. The more organized you are at interacting with your die-hard fans, the more effective they will be at spreading your gospel.

My favorite example of die-hard fanaticism comes from Pullman, Washington, where, despite having never hosted ESPN's *College GameDay*, Pullman's own Washington State University has become a fixture on the show. How? Each week the *GameDay* crew travels to the site of college football's biggest game, and every week Chris Fowler, Lee Corso, and Kirk Herbstreit do their thing in front of a live mob of raucous, flag- and sign-waving fans. Remarkably, during every show, like clockwork, you will find a Washington State Cougars flag flying among those of the host and rival schools. This is not the brainchild of the Washington State sports marketing department. No, the idea to represent the school in front of a national audience came from and

involve your hardcore fan base in your communication strategy.

is being executed by die-hard fans of the university. By creating a network of fans and shipping out Cougars flags to local supporters across the country, the school has been represented on nearly every *College GameDay* broadcast since 2004. It's a great story and a testament to the dedication sports fans have for their teams.

"did we win? i was brushing my teeth."
—casual fan

Casual fans of a particular program tend to support the school in a much more subtle way, choosing to wear school gear for function versus fanaticism and usually only on or around gameday. Driving behind a casual fan, you can discern what school he or she attended or roots for, but only if you are making a concerted effort to find the one or maybe two rare and subtle pieces of university paraphernalia that adorn the car.

While die-hard fans force themselves to sit through the good and bad times, casual fans are usually only around for the good and are unlikely to fill seats during anything resembling a down year. As quickly as casual fans jump on the bandwagon during a successful season, they'll just as quickly lose interest at the first sign of struggle.

Casual fans are the equivalent of mainstream consumers. This group is made up of followers that let others influence and, in some cases, make their decisions. This is a very important point to understand. If a casual fan's friends are doing it, that person likely will too. As it relates to sports, if the casual fan's friends are getting excited about a particular athletic program, going to home games, and gathering during away games, the casual fan will soon follow suit, whether the person knows the quarterback, point guard, or starting pitcher's name or not. In the summer of 2013, Nielsen set out to determine whether or not Twitter activity drove increased tune-in rates for broadcast TV and whether or not broadcast TV tune-in then led to increased Twitter activity. According to Paul Donato, Nielsen's chief research officer, the company found that "a spike in TV ratings can increase the volume of tweets, and, conversely a spike in tweets can increase tune-in" (Nielsen,

2013). In simple terms, activity leads to influence on those members of your audience who need to feel safe when it comes to decision making; the more this group sees other people taking part in something, the more likely they are to take part themselves.

Casual fans are the late adopters of the sports world, choosing to wait for others to indicate when rooting is appropriate. Think about it this way: if the average consumer walked past two restaurants with the exact same menu, the exact same quality, and the exact same décor, the only difference being one was full and one was empty, that consumer will likely choose to eat at the restaurant that's packed. Why? Because it must be good if everyone else is doing it! The same lesson holds true for casual fans in regards to stadiums and arenas. If a casual fan had to choose between two programs with the same win-loss record—one with a consistently full, raucous crowd and the other barely filling 50 percent of its capacity—the casual fan is going to choose the former just about every time. The live experience plays a major role when dealing with and converting casual fans; clearly a jam-packed facility portrays a more enjoyable experience than the alternative.

When it comes to attracting the casual fan, it is vital that you fill your stadium at whatever cost. If you have to give tickets away until your demand matches your capacity, do it. Stadium attendance has a major impact on your program's perception. Fans are not the only individuals turned off by an empty arena. Blue-chip recruits who are used to playing in front of packed houses will expect more of the same in college. From a media standpoint, empty arenas make for bad television, which will adversely affect your exposure potential.

The casual fan segment's value comes in its sheer size. The casual fan and potential fan segments are typically the largest of the three groups (die-hard fans being the smallest), with casual fans providing for an easier transition to die-hard loyalists because of their existing affinity (however small it may be) for your program. If you tell a transcending story that reaches this group, combined with an engaging and memorable experience, you will be well on your way to building a winning and profitable program.

"i just want to see a good game."
—potential fan

Potential fans are those fans of a particular college sport who have yet
to pledge their allegiance to any one program. Watch a college football
game, and you'll see a stadium filled with alumni and one-time potential
fans turned current fans. To think college football stadiums or basketball
arenas are filled to the brim with current and former students is unrealistic.
Your program needs to attract and convert those fans who have no inherent
connection with your school or program. Potential fans range from children
all the way up to adults, from fans who did not attend college to transplants
who moved to your state and want to root for a local team. The fact is, as
stadiums and arenas get larger, you need these fans to fill your seats.

"i want the best for my child."
—mom

Much like fans, parents can be broken down into three categories: parents
of potential student athletes (impacting your sport's performance), parents
of prospective students (impacting attendance and overall university health),
and parents of prospective fans (impacting attendance, fan-base size,
and program perception), all of which have a hand in how successful your
program is.

Parents have an incredible amount of influence when it comes to the
young adults essential to growing your fan base, not to mention the impact
parents can have come signing day, a day in which high school student
athletes choose where they will play in college. In many cases parents have
as much of a say in where a prospective athlete goes as the athlete himself
or herself. Having parents on your side can give you an invaluable leg up on
the competition. It becomes very important to be able to take your professional hat off and put your parental hat on. What would you want a program
to provide your son or daughter? Think about it at the most basic level and
incorporate that thinking into your game plan.

"yo, those uniforms are sick."
—recruit

Recruits and potential student athletes are clearly the heart and soul of any program. Looking at the Athletic Program Life Cycle, recruiting success can be directly correlated to program success. It's that relationship that makes this group of individuals so important. Everything you do to build relationships with fans, parents, media, and the like is ultimately done in an effort to impress this group of highly skilled athletes.

Because this group has become savvy with both technology and advertising, how you tell your story becomes just as important as what your story is.

In the fall of 2013, the Oregon State football administration took to Twitter to connect with this group. The Oregon State coaching staff leveraged Twitter's popularity with teenagers by coming up with an episodic program they called *Tweet Film Tuesday*. High school athletes were encouraged by Head Coach Mike Riley, through his own Twitter account: "Tweet your HL [highlight] link to #GoBeavs and our Recruiting Dept will choose 10 to evaluate." This was an ingenious and authentic way to reach high school athletes where they spend a majority of their time. This is a great example of fishing where the fish are. Assistant Director of Player Personnel Ryan Gunderson summed it up best when he said, "We have to think outside the box. If we do what everyone else is already doing, it's not going to be effective" (*Oregonian*, October 23, 2013).

❝ we have to think outside the box. if we do what everyone else is already doing, it's not going to be effective. **❞**

(ryan gunderson)

"i need something to write about."
—media

Perhaps the most influential of all of your targets is the media. In many ways, it's this group that controls the success or failure of your story. There are a few things to understand when it comes to the media. First, it's their job to report on the news, which means they need stories—and you have stories. Second, they are extremely busy; many of these outlets cover multiple sports, and even those blogs covering a single sport are, in many cases, still reporting on an entire country of programs. This group is overwhelmed, and in the age of social media, it's very difficult to keep up. Help them. Bring stories *to them*, and they will oftentimes return the favor by pushing your content out to their thousands, sometimes millions, of followers. Third, every media outlet is looking for the exclusive. One way to differentiate yourself as a news source is to be the first to break the story. That means, oftentimes, you can offer first-release rights to key media for premium placement in return.

Get to know your media partners. Ask them what they like, what they don't like, what they need, and how you can help. The more you understand and can put yourself in their shoes, the more effective you will be at leveraging their space.

the diffusion of ideas

Each member of your audience, from media to recruits, plays a unique and important role in disseminating your story. Geoff Moore, author of *Crossing the Chasm*, used the idea *diffusion curve*, a theory popularized by sociologist Everett Rogers in the 1960s, to do an excellent job of visualizing how ideas spread.

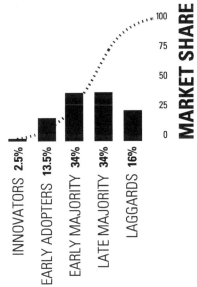

According to Moore, ideas—or in our case, stories—begin at the left of the curve with the more influential "innovators" and "early adopters" and end with "laggards," the last to adopt an idea. The x-axis along the bottom outlines each segment and size of a given population that an idea flows through, while the y-axis represents the rate and level of adoption.

This theory has stuck with me since I was first introduced to it in college, and it has influenced much of my work since. It's a theory that has survived the test of time and can be adapted and applied to any program looking to carve out a unique space in the NCAA landscape. By replacing the theory's population segments with our own key targets, you can begin to see how and what it will take for your story to stick.

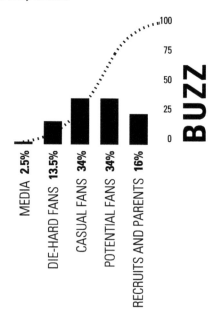

While the definitions of the first four segments in the diffusion curve match our own targets, the last segment, laggards, does not. In our case, the role of laggard is played by recruits and parents. Laggards have little to no opinion of leadership, which is very much contrary to what a high school blue-chip athlete represents among your core audience; however, the timing does indeed match. Recruits and parents are typically the last and most difficult to convince because of their level of investment and the impact their decision can have on their own futures, which far outreaches the impact of the other segments. At the end of the day, the media have the most influence and reach among your core audience, and their reporting can act as a catalyst for a story dissemination process that starts with die-hard fans and then moves through to casual and potential fans. Finally, after everyone has adopted your story as his or her own and the buzz has reached its peak, you are much more likely to convince your eighteen-year-old recruiting target to join your program.

RECAP CH**2** WRITING YOUR STORY

INFLUENCING PERCEPTION STARTS WITH A GREAT STORY

MAC
MADE YOU FEEL ASHAMED OF YOUR PC AND CONSIDER A CAREER IN GRAPHIC DESIGN.

MARLBORO
MADE YOU FEEL LIKE LESS OF A MAN IF YOU SMOKED ANYTHING ELSE.

ALI
MADE YOU THINK HE IS THE GREATEST BOXER OF ALL TIME.

A COUPLE OF NCAA BRANDS HAVE STARTED TO WRITE THEIR OWN STORIES...

OREGON
FOOTBALL

THE COLLEGE FOOTBALL PROGRAM OF THE FUTURE

DUKE
BASKETBALL

THE COLLEGE BASKETBALL PROGRAM DRIVEN BY EXCELLENCE ON AND OFF THE COURT

BEFORE YOU WRITE A STORY THAT SHAPES YOUR FUTURE

DIG DEEP INTO YOUR **PAST** AND **PRESENT**. LOOK AT...

RIVALS	TRADITIONS	LOCATION	PEOPLE
WHAT MAKES YOU DIFFERENT FROM YOUR RIVALS?	WHAT'S THE STORY BEHIND EACH OF YOUR TRADITIONS?	WHAT MAKES YOUR CITY OR STATE SPECIAL?	DOES YOUR PROGRAM HAVE A REVERED COACH OR PLAYER FROM THE PAST?

YOUR STORY MUST BE
SIMPLE. QUICK. CONSISTENT. RELEVANT.

8"

THE ATTENTION SPAN OF
THE AVERAGE HUMAN IS
EIGHT SECONDS.

**GET TO
THE POINT**

2

REPEATING THE NAME OF A
NEW ACQUAINTANCE TWICE
ALOUD IMPROVES YOUR
CHANCE OF RECOLLECTION.

**BE
CONSISTENT
& FREQUENT**

92%

92% OF PEOPLE TRUST RECOMMEN-
DATIONS FROM FRIENDS OR FAMILY
ABOVE ALL OTHER FORMS OF
ADVERTISING.

**GIVE THEM
SOMETHING
TO TALK
ABOUT**

WHO
IS READING
YOUR STORY

FANS
PARENTS
RECRUITS
MEDIA

CH2 HOMEWORK

✦ What is it about your sport that keeps fans coming back? What makes it special?

....

✦ What makes your athletic program unique? What is your program's essence? Who from your school's past or present embodies that essence?

....

✦ What are the key differences or similarities between you and your fiercest rival?

....

✦ What do people in your community love most about your city or town?

....

♦ What traditions does your program currently engage in? Where did they originate? What is the meaning behind each?

....

♦ What is your athletic program's story? Fill in the points below.

target

frame of reference

story

reasons to believe

values

....

♦ What are you currently doing to influence, engage, and draw in your target fans, parents, athletes, and media?

....

notes

. . . .

3
telling
your story

one chance to make a first impression

JEREMY DARLOW

At this point you should have a very firm grasp on what makes your program unique and what your brand's story is. If not, hold off on reading ahead until you do.

What follows are many of the most common and effective ways to activate a brand and tell stories. However, there is no use in thinking about activation if your strategy and story are not already in place. That is a common mistake I see in brand marketing — skipping steps. Activation is the fun part, and because of that there is a tendency to jump straight into coming up with new and unique tactics, with the hopes of finding that silver bullet that turns a brand around or gets everyone talking. The problem with leaping without looking is twofold. First, without building equity in a story that leads to activation, the activation itself can seem forced and inauthentic, which opens you up for ridicule and criticism rather than celebration of a great idea. You only get one chance at a first impression, and how you develop and roll out your story is no different. Second, without a plan or a story that carries you beyond the moment, any momentum you generate can go away in an instant, no matter how successful the tactic is. If you're not prepared to sustain the conversation, you're not building your brand.

Now, all that being said, if you are satisfied with your story and you have a sound strategy, you are absolutely ready to begin building your activation plan. Your objective in this phase is to crystallize your position through the moments and techniques you choose to execute. Within each activation point or tactic below, you will find examples on how to do just that.

This is the fun part. This is where you tell your story.

if you're not prepared to sustain the conversation, you're not building your brand.

consistency
+ frequency

---

success

By now you've spent hours upon hours coming up with a story that truly and genuinely defines your program's identity. It's time to put it into action. In marketing terms that means inserting your story into every (and I mean *every*) piece of outbound communication or point of contact between you and your target consumers. From the music your fans listen to while they're on hold with your athletic department to the billboard you erect in your rival's backyard, everything should start with and contribute to your brand story.

When it comes to telling your story, two things are key in making it stick: consistency and frequency. The more people come into contact with the same, consistent message (especially in different places), the more likely they are to remember that message and, assuming it's a good one, believe it. Consistency and frequency are two crucial pillars to any successful brand story. Howard Schultz is often credited as saying: "Authentic brands don't emerge from marketing cubicles or advertising agencies. They emanate from everything a company does." Emphasis there on the word *everything*. Keep that in mind while you read the rest of this chapter and begin formulating your marketing plan.

❝ authentic brands (...) emanate from everything a company does. **❞**
(howard schultz)

identification, please

What they see is what you get—meaning what your audience sees with their own eyes is what in many cases forms their opinions of who you are and what your program stands for. It's up to you to use those visual cues to your advantage.

put a logo on it

Your logo is the most recognizable piece of your brand identity, and as such it should reflect the values of your program and the story you are trying to tell. Take a look around the room right now and find your logo. Examine it closely. Now let me ask you this: if a high school senior ten states away were to look at that logo, in its current form, how would that kid feel? Would that logo elicit any of the emotions you are trying to produce with your brand story? If your answer is no, you may want to consider rebranding your program and athletic department. Your logo is a great place to start the rebranding process.

When it comes to number of logos, one is enough. Do everything you can to build a single logo that works for all of your needs. The reason? Consistency and frequency. Again, the more you use the same consistent logo, the more recognizable it becomes to fans, media, and recruits—especially those outside of your state who may not realize your team exists or come into contact with your story as much as they do their local teams'.

In 2001, the University of Oregon began a rebranding process that started with a logo built to reflect its new brand story as the team of the future (my words, not its). Rather than leading with their mascot, the standard for many schools, the Ducks chose to create a sleek, modern logo that reflected where they were going as a brand. The *O* logo (*O* for Oregon) immediately made its way to the stands, with fans today making hand gestures in the shape of the Oregon *O* for the same purpose fans at the University of Texas use two fingers pointing to the sky to represent the Longhorns. Because its design is so simple, you can almost see that Oregon *O* from space. Okay, if you're a literal person, that's not true, but the simplicity of the logo does allow for easy identification from a distance, another benefit the university no doubt took into account during the design process.

Do not overthink your logo. Your objective is to create a visual identifier that is easy to read and easy to remember, just like the Oregon *O*.

what's your favorite color?

With color, as with your logo, pick one and own it. I'm not saying lose your secondary color—that's a part of your school and your tradition. I'm saying lead with one color. If you're Michigan, lead with blue or maize but not both. I know that might sound like blasphemy to a Wolverine, but the image of over one hundred thousand fans all dressed in the same color filling the stands makes an impression on the media, recruits, and fans. A stadium or arena filled with fans dressed in multiple colors or multiple shades of a color looks like any other gameday experience. It's not memorable. When Penn State executes its whiteout nights at Beaver Stadium, it brings tears to my eyes. Imagine an eighteen-year-old recruit walking into a stadium filled with one hundred and ten thousand screaming fans all dressed in white; the visual impact alone can take your breath away.

That's a difficult atmosphere to

a stadium filled with fans dressed in multiple colors looks like any other gameday experience. it's not memorable.

turn your back on if you're a young, impressionable recruit. It's an experience a fan won't want to miss, no matter the opponent. Not to mention that it makes for beautiful television. Anything you can do to convince the power networks to play your games on TV is worth the effort and investment. Color also provides you with an additional point of brand differentiation. Consider North Carolina blue, Nebraska red, and Texas burnt orange. When you see a football or baseball stadium filled with fans in any of these three colors, chances are your mind goes to one of these schools. Each has done a tremendous job of building equity and ownership in its color. North Carolina and Texas specifically have done well in choosing colors that are unique to their universities. The light blue of North Carolina and burnt orange of Texas are distinctive versions of the more common blue and orange other schools fashion their programs in. Each is a subtle change in shade, but it makes a world of difference when it comes to ownership. From there, both Nebraska, by promoting the moniker Big Red, and North Carolina, with its Carolina Blue, have gone so far as to brand their colors. Each one of these universities offers lessons in how to make color part of your brand identity.

whose line is it, anyway?

If you're going to have a tagline or motto, once again, make sure there is a reason for it and that that reason comes from your story. In fact, that motto should be the shortest, most concise elevator pitch for your brand story there is. Seth Godin said it best on his blog: "Start with a slogan. But don't bother wasting any time on it if you're merely going for catchy. Aim for true instead" (2012). In my experience, fluffy marketing is no marketing, especially when it comes to building a long-term brand. In everything you do, every time you speak, there needs to be a reason and an objective that ladders up to a bigger picture. How does your motto relate to what you want your program to be? A motto can have a great impact on how people see your team, how they remember your team, and what they remember it for. However, the motto needs to have a reason for being, and your line needs to be a part of a longer journey.

For me, the two most important elements of a successful tagline are:

① Is it simple and easy to understand? Will someone comprehend what you are trying to say in the split second it takes to read it?

If your line requires any deciphering at all, you've lost your audience. With Apple's "Think different" motto, you had a simple idea in a small package. It doesn't take a lot to understand what the company is trying to say, even without visuals.

② Is the motto telling the brand's story? Will someone be able to read the tagline and understand what makes that brand special?

In Apple's case, I believe the answer to be yes. Apple was saying, quite literally, "We're different, we're not like everyone else, and we're not for the conformist." Bye-bye, sheep. That irreverent attitude has resonated with "creative" crowds all over the world, leading to Apple becoming one of the strongest and most successful brands of our time.

> **"** start with a slogan. but don't bother wasting any time on it if you're merely going for catchy. aim for true instead. **"**
> (seth godin)

brand before beauty

Any and all marketing materials produced by your athletic department (or your agency of record) must clearly, concisely, and consistently tell your brand story. But you have to be careful here. It's very easy to let your agency take you down a creative path that looks amazing in print, on TV, or online but actually does nothing to help tell your brand story or build your brand for the long term.

The late David Ogilvy, considered by many to be the father of advertising, is often quoted as saying the consumer's decision to buy or not to buy is based on "the content of your advertising, not its form." Agencies are not invested in your university like you are. They are invested in their own brand, and they want to win awards. Rightfully so. But award-winning creative isn't always the best thing for you; in fact, more often than not, it doesn't help.

Marketing is about being consistent, frequent, and in this case literal, and literal isn't always fun or sexy. But it can often be the most effective way to get your point across. The minute your audience has to figure out what that beautiful piece of art is supposed to mean, your campaign is dead and your investment is lost. Stay strong and on course, and remember that many creative agencies are filled with artists who look for the beautiful before the brandable.

> **❝ the content of your advertising, not its form. ❞** (david ogilvy)

fashion week

When it comes to influencing your current fans, potential fans, and recruits, look no further than the athletes who take the field, court, or pitch. Trends start here. Your fans will wear the color the players wear. Your fans will wear the gear the players wear. Your fans want to be your players; as such, what your players do carries a tremendous amount of weight. Your athletes give the ultimate validation to your story.

designing your book cover

"Style is a way to say who you are without having to speak." This is a quote often attributed to Rachel Zoe, an American fashion stylist and designer known for her work with celebrities and her own reality TV show on Bravo, *The Rachel Zoe Project*. Bottom line, she knows fashion—and uniforms, love them or hate them, are fashion. Style is a brand identifier and a story-teller. Uniform design can go a long way in making your story feel authentic and genuine.

For instance, if you're trying to tell a story about a team made up of blue-collar, lunch pail–carrying athletes yet your uniforms look like something fresh off a Milan runway, people aren't going to believe you. Those two ideas do not align, and suddenly your story feels inauthentic. It won't stick.

style is a way to say who you are without having to speak. (rachel zoe)

Uniforms are, in essence, your packaging or your book cover, and they are one of the first things people will use to judge and label your team in their minds. People say, "Don't judge a book by its cover," but we do anyway. That's what will happen with your team and your uniforms. If you want your brand story to stick, your uniforms need to work seamlessly with and contribute to that story. When people think blue-collar football, they think Penn State, not Oregon. Uniforms tell stories.

> **if you want your brand story to stick, your uniforms need to work seamlessly with and contribute to that story.**

In fact, you won't find two more opposite approaches to uniform design than those of the Oregon Ducks and Penn State Nittany Lions football programs. On one hand you have Oregon, who has made a name for itself by creating the most polarizing, albeit technologically advanced, uniforms in the game today. The number of uniform combinations the program can wear seems to be endless and has become a story in itself. Oregon has used uniform design to bring attention to its program and crystallize its story. As a program the school is constantly looking to the future, and its uniform strategy is no different. On the other hand, you have Penn State, whose uniform is a tribute to the past. Penn State has perhaps the simplest uniform design in the country and has resisted the urge to change, despite pressure from its more progressive counterparts. Penn State football has always adopted a blue-collar, substance-over-style mentality, and its uniforms have told that story for years. Each brand, in very different ways, has used uniform design to bring its story to life.

color coding

I sound like a broken record here, but color is a tactic you'll use to build your brand across the board, and being strategic with uniform color becomes especially important. Your fans are going to associate your team with the color they wear to play, which means you can do all you want to push a color in your ad campaign, but if that particular color is not worn prominently on the field or court, it's not going to stick. If you want a color to stick, make it the primary color of your uniform. If you're pushing green, your uniform better be green. It's not enough simply to have green in the uniform. For this to work, green must be the primary color.

what's in a name?

Whether or not to have names on the backs of your uniforms may seem small, but it can go a long way in corroborating your story. Everything matters. If you're a program that preaches "we versus me" and another favorite sports cliché of mine, "It's what's on the front of the jersey, not the back," then it makes sense to remove names from your uniforms. That minor design change supports the story you're trying to tell. If you want people to believe what you're saying, you have to go all the way with that idea. Everything matters. You can't half-ass anything when it comes to building a brand. In 2012, Penn State football made headlines simply by putting names on the backs of its jerseys during an early-season game against Ohio University, something it hadn't done in the 125-year history of the team. Everything matters when it comes to telling your story.

Not having names on the backs of your jerseys means something. Having names on the backs of your jerseys means something. If you establish a position for your program and you stick with it, those little things that contribute to who you are become big, feel sacred, and grow to be part of your DNA. Penn State learned that lesson firsthand.

Did I mention, *everything matters*?

you're a sheep—for now

At this point, designing outlandish uniforms is old news. Yes, it still garners coverage, and if it fits your brand story and your position, then I encourage you to look at ways to create buzz through your uniforms. Distinctive uniforms have become a cost of entry into big-time college sports in some ways. However, it's time we as marketers find that next on-field differentiator. If everyone is designing new uniforms and every school has a hundred different variations to choose from, no one is unique. What made Oregon's uniform story so effective was the fact that the school took uniform design to extreme levels and was the first and only school to do it. The question becomes, what's next? What can be done with cleats, socks, gloves, mouth guards? Having worked on countless uniform launches in my time at adidas, I know for a fact that there are other areas of opportunity in which a team can make a statement. Are you brave enough to be first?

cold shoulders

In 2013, adidas Basketball unveiled the NBA's first modern short-sleeve jersey and short uniform system. Adidas called the full package the adizero NBA Short Sleeve Uniform System, which featured "the first ever super lightweight stretch woven short with maximum ventilation for player comfort" while the jersey included "armhole insets with 360-degree stretch fabric

people should love what you're doing or hate what you're doing; if people are indifferent, you've failed.

that facilitates free range of motion for the arms and shoulders." There were absolutely performance benefits to the uniform system in both the pants and the jersey, but what garnered attention and drove conversation were the sleeves. Adidas took a risk, and the reward was conversation. People either loved or hated the sleeves, and to me that's a win. Either way, fans and media were talking about adidas Basketball. People should love what you're doing or hate what you're doing; if people are indifferent, you've failed.

super bulldogs

College baseball has its own culture moment, the College World Series (CWS) in Omaha, Nebraska. The CWS features the final eight teams vying for a national championship. In 2013, adidas sponsored five of the eight CWS participants. As the head of brand and digital marketing for adidas Baseball at the time, it was my job to make sure people knew about it.

In partnership with our product and design teams, we rolled out a slew of throwback uniforms that our programs wore either during batting practice or during the games themselves. Because of the scale and inherent buzz surrounding the moment, we were able to garner extensive coverage from our key baseball media.

But it was a different story that broke through that year. We leveraged the event to unveil our newest adizero baseball cleat and lead color. The cleat itself was charcoal with neon-yellow highlights. You couldn't miss it in the stands or on TV.

The cleat's color combination didn't match the university colors of any of our participating schools—but that was the point. If that cleat were "colored up" to align with each team's uniform, it would have gotten lost. Neither adidas nor our schools would have received credit for it in the media.

Instead, thanks to the Mississippi State Bulldogs, who agreed to wear the cleats during the entirety of the CWS, we had people talking throughout the event. Like in the Notre Dame uniform launch example referenced at the beginning of step 1, the older Mississippi State alumni were not fans, but more important, the MSU players, media, and high school baseball players from all over the country loved them. We achieved what we set out to accomplish—adidas Baseball was the talk of the 2013 College World Series. In September of the same year, Nielsen published a study around the engagement patterns of Twitter users while watching television. The study reported that from a mix of fifty-nine cable and broadcast programs, 70 percent of Twitter activity came during the actual programming itself, with 30 percent coming during commercials (Nielsen, September 18, 2013). That data would seem to suggest that in-game "earned" disruption becomes just as valuable, if not more valuable as it relates to social engagement, as paid media. It puts major emphasis on product that gets people talking.

If you're going to break through the clutter, you have to be willing to break the rules and be bold. The Bulldogs were eager to take part, and they carried that audacious attitude to the field, cruising through the preliminary rounds and reaching the final three-game series for a chance at the title against fellow adidas school UCLA.

Must have been the shoes.

if you're going to break through the clutter, you have to be willing to break the rules and be bold.

tell me something I don't know

In the world of branding, be it product, services, or athletic programs, public relations is invaluable. PR exposure can take your brand story from a perceived narrative to reality in a very short period of time. The bottom line is you can't believe everything you read or hear on TV—but most of us do. If it's in the news, people usually assume it to be true. Also, PR usually doesn't cost a lot of money. Bonus. Never underestimate the power of the media to make or break a program.

the iowa way

To demonstrate this point, let's take a look at the University of Iowa wrestling program. Imagine ESPN does a story on Iowa wrestling during the heart of the season. The story revolves around the idea that the program is made up of blue-collar, lunch pail–carrying, hardworking young men who carry themselves the right way (no doubt a brand story the university could be telling already). Now imagine the impact such a story can have on the people of Iowa who grow up choosing between two schools: Iowa State University and the University of Iowa. Those are admirable qualities that would make any citizen of the great state of Iowa proud. Quite frankly, these are attributes I myself have already projected onto the University of Iowa program based on my own perception that the entire state of Iowa is filled with individuals who approach life in a similar way (key word: *perception*). This story may only reinforce that perception outside of the state; however, where the important impact takes shape is within Iowa. As I said, individuals in Iowa grow up rooting for either Iowa State University or the University of Iowa. Through a story on ESPN, the University of Iowa suddenly becomes the program that best represents what's good about the state and what many of its citizens take pride in embodying. Choosing a school in Iowa just got a lot easier.

Now let's say this story is immediately followed up by a paid-media campaign executed by the university that portrays the team just as ESPN made them out to be. The university is now reinforcing that message and providing fans of the program something to identify with and root for beyond wins and losses. Public relations combined with a focused brand story can be extraordinarily effective. The story alone may not be enough; remember, it's consistency and frequency that lead to reality. Striking while the iron is hot is not only important following landmark victories, it's also important following key public relations wins.

striking while the iron is hot is not only important following landmark victories, it's also important following key public relations wins.

brands defenses win championships

put media on speed dial

It's important to keep the local, regional, and national media abreast of what is happening with your program. Whether it's an event you're putting on or a feel-good story, if the press doesn't know about it, it's not going to get covered. And unless you're a national power, they will rarely come to you to get a story. Develop a press kit (what you include in that kit and its physical or digital form is up to you) that educates the media on your brand story and what makes your program unique. Be diligent about sending out your kits. If your budget doesn't allow you to bring in a full-time public relations manager, develop an internship program and assign press release responsibilities for individual sports to your interns. It's great experience for them and keeps your program top of mind with the media.

get creative in how you deliver your news.

Get creative in how you deliver your news. The more the media are bombarded with pitches for stories, the more important it is to be different upon delivery. The physical package in which the media receives your news is a lever to pull to get them excited. At adidas we used this approach consistently whenever we had what we considered to be newsworthy content. When we launched the first signature cleat for Robert Griffin III (RGIII) in November of 2013, we did so around Veterans Day because he grew up in a military household and credits what he learned then with who he is now. Our product team went so far as to design the shoe in military camouflage to honor our troops. It was then our job to take that story to the media in a way that would capture their attention. Rather than simply shipping the shoes in a traditional shoe box along with a printed release, we told the story through the actual packaging it was delivered in. The cleat arrived the morning of the game in an authentic military ammo kit spray painted with the adidas logo and personalized with the media contact's name. The kit included the cleat, dog tags, and a message from RGIII thanking the media for their support of the cause. By telling the story through the kit, the media not only covered the product launch, they covered the box and its contents as well. This gave the cleat more context and helped tell the military story we set out to tell. It also became one of the more fulfilling brand launches I've ever had the privilege to lead.

special delivery

In 2012, adidas launched a new uniform for Notre Dame's Shamrock Series, a tradition in which the Irish play a home game off-site against a marquee opponent. In this case that opponent was the University of Maryland and the location was Washington, DC.

To break the story to our key media outlets, my PR counterpart, Michael Ehrlich, and I developed a specially designed package that included an authentic jersey, a helmet plated with 14k gold flakes, and a vial of shavings from the famous Notre Dame Golden Dome.

The box, made of real wood, became as much of a story as the uniform itself, garnering coverage from the likes of Erin Andrews and ESPN, among others. As Michael said to me following the project, "In today's media landscape, when telling a brand story, it is extremely beneficial to go beyond using the traditional PR materials such as a press release, photography, and a YouTube video. By creating a media seeding kit, brands give reporters and influencers the opportunity to see their story in the flesh, create unique content, and share on their social channels. This not only extends your story but also continues to build relationships with key media stakeholders."

I couldn't have said it better myself. If you Google *College Football Uniforms*, you will get millions of results. New uniforms are passé; there's nothing new about them. In order to gain the interest of national media and the masses, your uniform needs to come with a story, and that story should align with the identity you are trying to build for your program.

your quarterback needs media training

It's important to remember that most of your school's communication actually comes straight from your players, coaches, and the administration via interviews before, during, and after the game. With that in mind, it's crucial that both your players and your coaches are mouthpieces for your brand story. If they are not living, breathing ambassadors for the brand you are trying to create, no one will believe you, and your story won't stick. Invest in media training; educate your players and coaches on how to speak on camera as well as what to say. It will pay huge dividends long term.

own your local newsstand

Season preview magazines and newspapers have become big business and seem to grow more and more popular every year. More important, these periodicals have taken a large piece of the preseason newsstand share of voice, which to you means getting a player or coach on these magazine covers will drive a great deal of awareness and give the perception of a major program within a specific region or even nationally (many of the magazine covers are regionalized to drive local sales). These outlets also come with online versions of their magazines, which offer your program additional exposure.

Much of what we speak of today is low-hanging fruit, and this is no different. Put someone in charge of managing this relationship and push for as many covers as you can. Offer exclusive interviews, content, and access to coaches and players—whatever it takes to get these covers. These magazines need content, and your program needs exposure. Make a deal.

Another advantage of these magazines is that TV and radio media read them. I know that because I listen to too much sports radio and I watch too much *SportsCenter*, and they often interview authors of these magazines, like Phil Steele, owner of *Phil Steele's College Football Preview*, one of the biggest preview magazines. But this is an important point: if the media, the keepers of perception in a lot of ways, are reading and believing what is said in these pages, it's crucial for you to get your program featured—and not just in the typical one- or two-page preview. I'm talking about garnering incremental coverage. Every year these magazines highlight one or two coaches or programs, giving those schools additional exposure in the magazine. If I'm a regional sports reporter and during the season prior I saw ESPN highlight Iowa basketball's blue-collar mentality, then saw billboards everywhere I went that told that same story, only to read in this year's *Phil Steele's Preview Magazine* similar dialogue on the team, I'm going to believe it, and I'm going to start preaching it myself to my thousands of listeners.

We're human, and we're affected by these things. The more we see something, the quicker we are to believe. Don't let these opportunities pass without pitching for coverage.

the more we see something, the quicker we are to believe.

build your own johnny heisman

A Heisman campaign—or any player-of-the-year campaign, for that matter—is risky. You never know what attention can do to a player, nor can you predict if a player gets hurt, but if you build a campaign and that player does do well, the exposure for your program is priceless. Take Texas A&M and the 2012 Heisman campaign it ran around Johnny Manziel's freshman season. At the time Manziel's buzz was on the rise, but it wasn't until the Aggies started promoting their prized freshman that Manziel became a serious part of the discussion, ultimately becoming the first freshman to win the award. I don't think it's a coincidence. Voters are human and can be swayed by hype. It happens consistently by way of big individual game performances or even spectacular single plays. But unless you tell voters and give them reason to vote for your guy, they may never even think of doing so.

In today's digital world, it's not difficult to get the word out about a potential player-of-the-year candidate. Social media offers you the platform to get the nation talking about your player and your program. Build a campaign around your star, tie it to your brand story, and cross your fingers. According to sports blog *Deadspin*, Texas A&M received $740 million in pledges and gifts the year after Manziel began starting for the Aggies. The previous year, when A&M was in the Big 12, the university's fund-raising intake was just $181 million. Research conducted by an A&M contractor shows Manziel winning the Heisman produced more than 1.8 million media impressions, which translates into $37 million in media exposure for the school (Texas A&M Athletics, January 2013).

1.8M

Research conducted by an A&M contractor shows Manziel winning the Heisman produced more than 1.8 million media impressions, which translates into $37 million in media exposure for the school.

do the right thing

Philanthropy support is a benefit on many levels. Most important, it's fulfilling to support a cause and help improve society in some way, and with that provide your program with invaluable PR. Three things are important to consider when thinking about what cause to support.

First, find a philanthropy that complements your brand story. For instance, supporting Farmers of America makes sense for the University of Iowa because of its blue-collar brand story and because of its geographic location. Farming is already an important piece of Iowa culture, giving citizens another reason to pledge allegiance to their Hawkeyes.

Second, make the media aware of your philanthropic efforts by building relationships with your local media affiliates. From there, provide your newfound partners with content through which they can tell your story, such as press releases accompanied by video and photography of your efforts. The media are so focused on the negative, it will almost be viewed as unexpected to see a program volunteering its time to support a cause. Involve your players and coaches as well as the community. Make it a joint effort. And don't wait until you make a bowl game like every other school does. That is so cliché at this point that it feels forced and inauthentic. Do it when no one expects it, and do it because you care.

Finally, support local school athletic programs. Helping your local school system develop its programs is a benefit to the future of your program, the sport, and the local school system. Consider helping build fields, stadiums, and facilities for local schools through physical labor. You likely have some of the strongest and most fit individuals in the community on your active rosters; encourage those among you to volunteer.

what happens in corvallis shouldn't stay in corvallis

Do not neglect the city or town your university resides in. The more attractive your program's hometown is to live in, the more attractive your university is to attend. If PR opportunities present themselves, take the initiative to get your town or city involved. Your town is a part of your program's DNA.

I went to school at Oregon State University in a small town called Corvallis, Oregon. The city itself is beautiful, and during my time there, it garnered a great deal of PR for being one of the safest and most environmentally friendly cities in the country. The problem was no one outside the city of Corvallis knew about it. Don't fall victim to the same gaffe. Your town can be just as much of a draw as your win-loss record.

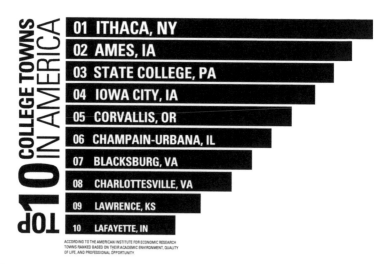

TOP 10 COLLEGE TOWNS IN AMERICA

01	ITHACA, NY
02	AMES, IA
03	STATE COLLEGE, PA
04	IOWA CITY, IA
05	CORVALLIS, OR
06	CHAMPAIN-URBANA, IL
07	BLACKSBURG, VA
08	CHARLOTTESVILLE, VA
09	LAWRENCE, KS
10	LAFAYETTE, IN

ACCORDING TO THE AMERICAN INSTITUTE FOR ECONOMIC RESEARCH
TOWNS RANKED BASED ON THEIR ACADEMIC ENVIRONMENT, QUALITY
OF LIFE, AND PROFESSIONAL OPPORTUNITY.

love thy neighbor

In many cases, rivalries are made up of two teams who are essentially the antithesis of one another, which can be a very good thing for you—if you have a tight brand story and positioning plan. Playing your rival can bring out what makes your team unique. Some of my favorite college football stories come out of rivalry games. One of the best originates with former Ohio State Coach Woody Hayes, who in 1968, with his Buckeyes up 50–14 on rival Michigan, late in the game promptly called for his team to go for two following a touchdown. Asked later why he went for two with such a comfortable lead, Hayes emphatically said, "Because I couldn't go for three." It's that genuine hatred that keeps college sports thriving and keeps programs in the news. It doesn't matter if Michigan is struggling or if Ohio State comes into the game with zero wins, the Michigan vs. Ohio State matchup is going to get covered by the media because of the history and animosity they have built up.

But don't be fooled. It's not all about on-field play when it comes to this rivalry or any other—it's marketing. That quote from Coach Hayes was genuine and uncontrived, making it a PR professional's dream. The more you market your rivalry as a game chock-full of intensity and pure hatred, the more the media will cover it. Imagine you are Don King promoting a prize fight. Your goal is to build as much hype around your rivalry as you can, and sometimes that means creating and manufacturing your own storylines. Leverage every medium you have to get people learning about your game and why it's so unique. Work with your rival—yes, your rival—to make your game against one another a household name. Do what you have to do to stir the pot, and from there, educate,

work with your rival to make your game against one another a household name.

educate, educate. From books to documentaries to interviews, find ways to get literature out there about your rivalry. Get fans, recruits, and media excited and talking about it. Building a rivalry, just like building your brand, is a marathon, not a sprint. A rivalry is what *you* make it.

seats taken

Another of my favorite rivalries in sports comes from the NFL, between the Jim Harbaugh–led San Francisco 49ers and the Pete Carroll–led Seattle Seahawks. I love it because the mind games and very public displays of dislike are not limited to players or coaches; no, this rivalry is so heated that even the ticket sales offices (!) are involved. And the media can't get enough.

During the 2013–2014 season, the 49ers and Seahawks third face-off was for the NFC Championship and for a chance to play in the Super Bowl. (This is not untypical for an interdivision rivalry. But what I enjoy most about this particular rivalry is the gamesmanship that fuels the game's fire.) Prior to the game on January 19, 2014, the Seattle Seahawk ticket office made it known that the team would not be selling tickets to individuals from the state of California. This is actually standard procedure, but as you can imagine, their making a point to announce it did not go over well with 49er fans and only furthered the animosity between the teams. This was an absolutely brilliant publicity stunt that got pickup from several of the major football blogs, taking hype for the game to another level.

COLLEGE FOOTBALL'S VS BEST RIVALRIES
ACCORDING TO SPORTING NEWS (2013)

ALABAMA	**01**	AUBURN
ARMY	**02**	NAVY
MICHIGAN	**03**	OHIO ST
TEXAS	**04**	OKLAHOMA
FLORIDA	**05**	GEORGIA
NOTRE DAME	**06**	USC
OREGON	**07**	OREGON ST
FLORIDA	**08**	FLORIDA ST
CLEMSON	**09**	SOUTH CAROLINA
UTAH	**10**	BYU

COLLEGE BASKETBALL'S VS BEST RIVALRIES
ACCORDING TO BLEACHER REPORT (2013)

DUKE	**01**	NORTH CAROLINA
LOUISVILLE	**02**	KENTUCKY
KANSAS	**03**	KANSAS ST
UCLA	**04**	ARIZONA
GEORGETOWN	**05**	VILLANOVA
INDIANA	**06**	PURDUE
KENTUCKY	**07**	FLORIDA
SYRACUSE	**08**	GEORGETOWN
MICHIGAN	**09**	OHIO STATE
DUKE	**10**	MARYLAND

put a sticker on it

Traditions are born from detail. Take helmet stickers in college football, for example. They're diminutive and subtle, but by being used across the vast majority of programs at one point or another, helmet stickers have become one of the sport's most celebrated traditions. There's a romance to customs like these that bring me, and millions of others, back to college sports every year. More important, they tell a story.

Evaluate your program and where you're taking it, and then ask yourself, "Do helmet stickers fit our brand?" And if they do fit your brand, what should they look like? If you're going to integrate helmet stickers or the equivalent for your sport, make sure the execution contributes to the story you are trying to tell. As is the case with names on your jerseys, it's details like these that make ideas stick. If you have existing traditions of your own, get them out there and seen. Use your PR department and put them in every piece of communication you send out around your program. Get the media to bear witness to (and even take part in) your traditions. Do whatever it takes to make them known. An unknown tradition is no tradition at all.

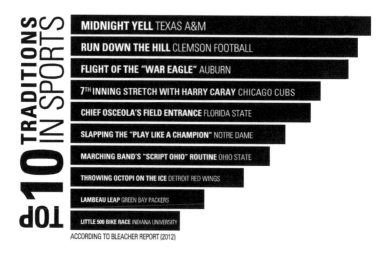

TOP 10 TRADITIONS IN SPORTS

MIDNIGHT YELL TEXAS A&M

RUN DOWN THE HILL CLEMSON FOOTBALL

FLIGHT OF THE "WAR EAGLE" AUBURN

7TH INNING STRETCH WITH HARRY CARAY CHICAGO CUBS

CHIEF OSCEOLA'S FIELD ENTRANCE FLORIDA STATE

SLAPPING THE "PLAY LIKE A CHAMPION" NOTRE DAME

MARCHING BAND'S "SCRIPT OHIO" ROUTINE OHIO STATE

THROWING OCTOPI ON THE ICE DETROIT RED WINGS

LAMBEAU LEAP GREEN BAY PACKERS

LITTLE 500 BIKE RACE INDIANA UNIVERSITY

ACCORDING TO BLEACHER REPORT (2012)

pull a stunt

I'll tell you right now, I *love* PR stunts. As a brand marketer, I constantly push my PR counterparts (I'm sure they love it) to create and manufacture stories rather than wait for stories to happen organically. PR is organic at times and manufactured during others. Create your own PR!

An excellent example of manufactured PR coverage is the story of Bruce Pearl, former Tennessee *men's* basketball coach, who decided to show his support for the women's basketball team one year by watching a Lady Vols game from the student section. Did I mention he was sans shirt and had painted his body orange? It brought tremendous coverage, and not only to the women's basketball program and the game that was being played. It also did an especially good job of making people aware of the Tennessee men's basketball program—no doubt Coach Pearl's objective. Love him or hate him, in this instance, he got the job done.

My favorite PR stunt, the one I use more than any to demonstrate the power of PR and manufactured stories, is the Heisman trophy campaign for Joey Harrington developed by the University of Oregon. Harrington was absolutely in the conversation at the time, but there is no doubt his public profile increased by leaps and bounds as a result of the media generated from the massive, $250,000 billboard the university erected in New York City reading, *Joey HEISMAN* (*The Wall Street Journal*, August 20, 2013). The University of Oregon took matters into its own hands and made absolutely sure its star quarterback and the university were at the forefront of any Heisman talk.

When opportunities for exposure arise, brainstorm ways in which you can magnify that exposure and garner press beyond the box score.

your logo—everywhere

Product placement is one of the more underutilized tactics that I see in college sports. Because of that and because of the influence celebrities have on our own consumer decision-making process, it could also be one of the most impactful. There's a reason major consumer product brands have full teams dedicated to getting their products seen on or used by key influencers: it truly influences the masses. Brad Pitt seen wearing a particular jeans brand can have a significant impact on sales for that manufacturer. The same can be said for college athletic programs. If Jay-Z is caught sporting a Rutgers hat at a club and later seen on the sideline during the school's next football game, suddenly one of the most influential individuals for thirteen-to-seventeen-year-olds across the nation is considered a Rutgers fan. And if Jay-Z likes Rutgers, then the high school athlete and student likes Rutgers.

they want to be like mike, and clay, and derek

One thing that became clear to me early on in my work in the sports world was the fact that high school athletes are heavily influenced by their heroes playing at the college and professional levels. Whether it is baseball, football, or basketball, the NBA, the NFL, or MLB, professional athletes can authenticate and sell a message, a school, or a product. That is exactly why brands like adidas, Nike, and Under Armour spend millions of dollars every year to sign endorsement deals with these icons. Fortunately for your program, at least in theory, your former athletes who make it to the professional level are more likely to support your program for free. When that happens, minds and perception can change.

You need to keep your celebrity alumni involved, engaged, and willing to support your program postgraduation. Think about a baseball program like Cal State Fullerton, which has a countless number of athletes playing in Major League Baseball today. Imagine if during every media interview with one of those athletes, each wore a bright blue and orange CSFU hat, ideally the same hat for each player to create repetition and recall with your target audience. Suddenly the perception is that CSFU has a ton of athletes in the majors, an idea not lost on a high school baseball player looking to sign with a school. The thing is, the average high school kid, athlete or not, doesn't research MLB rosters. Even though the Titans have a large number of former athletes playing in the majors, that fact is likely lost on most kids. It's up to the school to make that known. If I'm a kid and it feels like I see a Titans hat every time I watch a baseball interview on ESPN, suddenly I do think of CSFU as the program that sends the most players to the show.

Take this same approach when it comes to social media. Professional athletes are addicted to social media, especially Twitter. Knowing that, make sure you encourage your celeb alumni to call out your school every chance they get. Seed those athletes with new gear every time you launch a new uniform or new product. They should be the first people you call when you have something you want talked about online. Look for every connection you can.

jeremy darlow, oregon state university

It started as a *Monday Night Football* tradition that has since transitioned to Sunday night and has become a tool for building the reputation and enhancing the perception of college football programs across the country. What is it? Lineup introductions. Rather than having the commentators introduce the lineups of each team, *Monday Night Football* decided to let the players introduce themselves and the school they come from. It's that last part that's important. Each time a professional player says the name of your school, your program becomes more relevant in the minds of fans, potential recruits,

> **each time a professional player says the name of your school, your program becomes more relevant.**

and media. Make sure your former players are saying your school's name during these lineup intros, not their high school or middle schools, as some love to do.

Two universities have utilized this touch point to their advantage and as a result now have tangible, national stories to tell. Ohio State University alumni now playing in the NFL use the opportunity to introduce themselves as former players of "*The* Ohio State University." What does the *The* mean? No idea. The former Ohio Agricultural and Mechanical College changed its name to The Ohio State University in 1878, with *The* as part of its official name. I suppose it makes sense; OSU is the only Ohio State University in the country, and thus The Ohio State University. More important, what these players do by introducing themselves as former athletes of The Ohio State University is present the moniker to people outside the walls of the Columbus, Ohio, campus and create the perception that the OSU football program is in a class of its own, a fraternity for football's elite. It sounds overblown, but you have to understand we as human beings naturally want to be part of something bigger than us. This moniker established Ohio State as something more than just a school—it's a way of life and a culture. The result is a point of differentiation for the OSU program.

The second program to leverage this tool, arguably more effectively than Ohio State, is the University of Miami. The Hurricanes have one of the strongest professional football alumni bases of any college football program and, more important, what may be the most passionate alumni base. If there's a professional football player who played at the University of Miami, chances are he's representing his school. Former Hurricanes have made it a tradition to represent their school on *Sunday Night Football* by introducing themselves as alumni of not the University of Miami but "The U." It can be argued that it was this nationally televised forum that allowed the university to rebrand itself. Today, you will seldom hear about the University of Miami; instead, as former Hurricane great Michael Irvin says, "It's all about The U."

In 2013, *Sunday Night Football* had six telecasts reach over 25 million people. That's a national audience you cannot afford to miss out on (NBC Sports Group, December 31, 2013).

25M
in 2013, *sunday night football* had six telecasts reach over 25 million people.

brands defenses win championships

the *gameday* gang

ESPN has a monopoly on Saturday morning sports television in the fall, which is why the network's weekly show *College GameDay* deserves its own section. ESPN's college football pregame show averaged over 1.8 million national viewers in 2013 (*SportsBusiness Daily*, December 20, 2013). This is one of my favorite areas of opportunity in this entire book, and it's one of the quickest and cheapest ways to drive awareness and affect perception for your program. Football programs featured on this show are legitimized, either more so or for the first time. The best part is it's not just for football anymore. Basketball has earned its own show. Opportunities on these programs abound.

What you shouldn't do is say, "Well, we're not at a point where ESPN will visit our campus for a game." That's okay. Are they likely to visit a nearby rival anytime soon? If they are, you're in business. Think back to the Washington State College *GameDay* example, and you will realize that you can make an impression in front of millions watching the show without being involved in the host contest. If a nearby rival school is a part of *College GameDay*, rally your ambassador army, load up the buses, and make a statement in the crowd behind Lee Corso, Kirk Herbstreit, and the rest of the *GameDay* crew. Once your program gets on the winning track, you can start making serious pitches to ESPN to play host one weekend in the fall or winter.

who in the world is jared zabransky?

The video game industry is one of the strongest segments of the entertainment world. Its drivers are fourteen-to-thirty-five-year-olds, the perfect demo for building a healthy fan base. By 2015, experts expect global video game revenues to reach over $111 billion, a sizeable increase from the $78 billion reported in 2012 (Statista.com, 2014). Each year the releases of Electronic Arts' *Madden NFL and NCAA Football* create huge buzz online and in traditional media. Getting a player from your program on the cover of one of these games instantly gets you millions of impressions nationwide. Each release is prominently featured in major retailers like Target, Walmart, and Best Buy, not to mention the online, print, and television exposure. EA spends millions of dollars each year on advertising for its football releases, and the cover boy sits front and center in each campaign.

EA and the NCAA have since parted ways due to licensing issues, but there's too much money being left on the table to not think EA or another publisher will once again produce a college football game. When it does, that cover becomes gold to every program in the country, and the land grab will be fierce.

The amount of exposure for being on one of these game covers is price-less. After Boise State's miraculous victory over the University of Oklahoma in the Fiesta Bowl, Boise State Quarterback Jared Zabransky was awarded the cover of the subsequent *NCAA Football* release. Brad Larrondo, Boise State's senior assistant athletic director for promotions and marketing at the time, put the importance of the cover this way: "It's extremely big for us as an athletic department. It crosses generations by touching kids and adults… It's an incredible marketing opportunity" (*Idaho Statesman*, March 1, 2007).

Of video game players in the United States in 2013, 64 percent were under the age of 35, making video games a great place to attract new fans to your program (Statista.com, 2014).

uncle luke and his crew

One thing that's universal, no matter your age, gender, or ethnicity, is music. Music transcends our differences, and it can be very, very influential. Think about the influence 2 Live Crew had on the University of Miami in the '80s. It was a perfect storm for the Hurricanes (so to speak): at the moment "The U" turned the corner as a football program, Miami musician Luke Campbell and his group were blowing up the rap scene in South Florida—and they were doing it while wearing Hurricanes gear. The controversial nature of 2 Live Crew was a perfect fit for the equally controversial Hurricanes football team.

It was a match made in heaven, and it added to the Hurricanes mystique. Luke and the boys started showing up on the sidelines during games, and Miami started to own South Florida in recruiting. Its reach went national, leading to unmatched success on the field at the time.

Consider what music can do for your program. Look at two things:

1 **What local bands or artists can you reach out to? (If you have the resources, you can certainly go broader in your search, but local is a tie that makes sense and will be an easier sell to the artists.)**

2 **Which of those local acts match your brand story?**

Whether the University of Miami president at the time wants to admit it or not, 2 Live Crew fit the Hurricanes brand story at the time, and it took the program to a new level. If you're the University of Iowa telling a blue-collar story, look for a similar blue-collar, all-American musician or group to carry your torch.

What's the goal here? At the outset you're simply hoping for the members of the band to wear your paraphernalia. Having a hat show up on a stage can separate you from the competition locally and—if fortuitously that musician gets big enough and continues wearing your garb—nationally. How do you do it? Send them gear accompanied by a handwritten note from your head coach. It will mean more coming from the coach than a marketing suit. Be genuine, be real, and pull on the local heart strings; your success and their success benefit your state in similar ways.

tmz your sideline

Another approach to seeding is to invite artists and actors or actresses onto your campus during a televised sporting event. Rather than taking your brand to them, bring them to you. From LeBron James, Chris Paul, and Carmelo Anthony showing up on the sideline of a University of Oregon football game to Lil Wayne in the front row of Miami Heat basketball games, celebrities attending sporting events instantly puts those programs at a perceived elite level. Basketball and football are the obvious choices, but think about the impact a celebrity of that caliber can have by simply attending one of the other countless sports programs available to student athletes, like baseball or volleyball or soccer. It can be substantial in elevating your school and program.

clear logo placement, full hearts, can't lose

Around 2004, pundits started proclaiming everywhere they could that TV was dead. TV isn't dead. Far from it. In fact, TV *still* sets the tone with today's youth. I can't tell you how many times over my career I've heard from high school kids in focus groups who say, "We don't see you on TV. You need to make commercials." If you're on TV, you're legit; if you're not on TV but your direct competition is, you're JV to its varsity. Getting your brand on TV is huge, and it doesn't always mean signing a network deal or spending millions on a Super Bowl ad. Product placement in regularly scheduled TV programming can get you on TV and in front of millions of potential fans. In 2013, CBS's *The Big Bang Theory* averaged over 13 million viewers (Nielsen, 2013). Imagine getting your product placed on a show with that level of reach.

Look at the now-retired show *Friday Night Lights*. It was sport-specific to football, and it targeted teens, which made it a perfect avenue to speak to thirteen-to-seventeen-year-old football players and fans. How can you get your program represented on a show like that? To answer that, you first have to answer the question: "What's in it for *Friday Night Lights*?" Basically, why would producers want to put your school on their show? Think about what you have to offer—two things specifically: coaches and former players. Having Kevin Sumlin from Texas A&M or Earl Campbell as a former Texas football legend on the show adds credibility to the series and gives the Texas A&M University and University of Texas football programs a major advantage over the competition.

Think about the next *Friday Night Lights* or your sport's equivalent; what can you offer the show that will get you in? And be careful not to think your school is too small for something like this. Remember that these shows try to be as realistic as possible, and not every kid's going to North Carolina to play basketball. The second-leading scorer on the show's team might accept a scholarship at Tennessee Tech.

your neighborhood applebee's

There's a reason athletic departments and professional sports teams target families: get one person in the family on your side and you have a good chance of getting them all! It only makes sense to try and get your story into locations frequented by families. And what's one thing families do a lot of? Eat out. From 2002 to 2013, fast food industry revenues in the United States went from $138 billion to $199 billion, with experts expecting that number to increase to $210 billion by 2017 (Statista.com, 2014). Which makes restaurants a great place to tell your brand story. Find out which of your alumni owns and operates a restaurant, and feed them your school's paraphernalia and swag. But don't stop with alumni-owned establishments—get your brand up on the walls of as many restaurants as you can. If there are team flags flying outside a restaurant, your logo better be on one of them. If there's a restaurant that covers its walls in sports memorabilia, you better grab some of the stuff collecting dust in your stadium's basement and donate it. If you have a weekly coach's television or radio show, you better be streaming it live from one of the most popular restaurants in the state. Restaurants provide you with a platform from which to tell your story and the opportunity to gain fans by the handful versus one at a time.

these magic moments

Sports are events in and of themselves; however, it would be a mistake and a detriment to your brand if you relegated your focus entirely to gameday. There are countless opportunities outside of the actual gameday itself— even outside of the season—for you to build your brand and your fan base. Here are a few to consider for your program.

midnight scrimmages and the fans who love them

Football and basketball are year-round sports for most of the country, which means you can get fans involved in these particular programs outside of the traditional in-season months. In 2013, the University of Auburn reported a crowd of over eighty-three thousand in attendance to watch its football program's spring game (*SB Nation*, April 21, 2013). But football is not the only sport with a preseason culture moment. Midnight Madness in basketball provides an event before the season even begins in which fans want to be involved. Make it an experience, if not for the product on the court then for the families attending. Make it something families look forward to every year. Give people a reason to attend outside of the desire to see next year's team. The reality is the majority of your fans aren't hardcore enough to care about a scrimmage featuring next year's squad; however, if you give them added incentive to attend the event, what happens on the court becomes icing. Think in the same way when it comes to events like spring football games or recruiting dinners and pep rallies, which cover all sports.

records are meant to be remembered

Record-breaking moments can stay with a fan for life. But that level of impression is based on you and the experience you provide. Fans should walk away both recognizing history being made and feeling like they were a part of it. Your goal is to give your audience chills while at the same time showing your appreciation for the athlete who is breaking the record. If you have an athlete or team on the verge of history, be prepared. Have souvenirs ready to give out as people leave. Give them something to cherish the moment by, and they will never forget.

"speech!"

Number or jersey retirement ceremonies are great for a couple of reasons. One, they give you permission to reach out to your fan base again while giving families another activity to attend that's centered around your program. Two, they are very important to keep your alumni involved and feeling appreciated. We already talked about the benefit of professional athletes representing your school and your program simultaneously. The more you show appreciation to your alumni, the more likely they are to turn themselves into walking and talking billboards for you.

the more you show appreciation to your alumni, the more likely they are to turn themselves into walking and talking billboards for you.

there's no place like home

Like retirement ceremonies, new facility openings give you a valid reason to reach out to your fan base. Not only that, but you are adding value by giving your audience a first look at your new building. Just another excuse to throw a party for your most faithful fans.

remember where you came from

Local community support is key in convincing recruits and families of those recruits that your school is right for them. College towns are a big draw to athletes, but in order to create that college-town atmosphere, you're going to need to get your community to rally around your program. Getting your team out and helping in the community is a great way to get the locals on your side.

While you're winning over the locals at these events, make sure you're passing out swag with your program and school represented, things like window signs, house flags, car flags, anything a potential recruit may see on a visit (i.e., not something that will sit inside someone's house). Capitalize on that goodwill you have built with the local community, and give them the nudge they need to start visibly showing their support for the program.

don't forget to check the rearview

Keep your former students involved through sponsored tailgates and other athletics-related gatherings, like recruiting dinners or end-of-season award ceremonies put on by the university. By doing so, you'll keep your school and athletic program top of mind; with that come butts in seats and ultimately an increase in your fan base. At every touch point, provide this group with material to promote your program. Look back before you look forward.

look back before you look forward.

virtual reality bites

Digital marketing is a hot topic, and everyone wants a piece of it. For your purposes, it's an absolutely crucial space. You've got to fish where the fish are. One of your primary targets is the high school kid; because of that, the internet—specifically social networks and mobile marketing—become crucial to you. Outside of television, this is where you're going to find this kid. In 2013, 50 percent of all tweets around TV in the United States were about sporting events. That's a total of 492 million tweets. In addition, twelve of the top twenty most tweeted about TV broadcasts in 2013 were sporting events (Nielsen, 2014).

50%

in 2013, 50 percent of all tweets around tv in the united states were about sporting events. that's a total of 492 million tweets. in addition, twelve of the top twenty most tweeted about tv broadcasts in 2013 were sporting events.

mobile homes

You can't talk digital marketing without first talking about mobile. As of 2013, 91 percent of Americans owned cell phones. Of that 91 percent, six in ten accessed the internet using their mobile devices. More important, 85 percent of eighteen-to-twenty-nine-year-olds use their phones to go online (*New York Daily News*, September 17, 2013). The stats speak for themselves; our society, your recruits, and your fans are moving to mobile devices more and more. The under-thirty crowd represents the future of your program in all capacities, and they are very likely to be consuming your content on their phones.

85%

85 percent of eighteen-to-twenty-nine-year-olds use their phones to go online.

Let's not forget tablets, either. By 2018, experts are predicting that global shipments of tablets will exceed those of desktop and laptop computers by nearly 100 million units (Richter, March 1, 2014). Whether it's a dot-com experience, paid media, or social content, your story will not stick if it is not built and optimized for these devices. From this day forward, there should be no campaign, no news, no content released without accompanying mobile and tablet assets. This is the present and future; without it you'll be a thing of the past.

quality over quantity

Digital media is now a standard in the media mix, so much so that many companies without TV budgets put the majority of their money into the digital space. For those of you without big budgets, I suggest building your online social presence now. By doing so, you're essentially eliminating some of the need to advertise on other channels because you're building a community of the individuals you want to speak to, anytime you want to, by simply posting to your accounts. These social networks have all become modern-day customer relationship tools. Having been focused on digital marketing in addition to my brand marketing responsibilities at adidas, I'm very fortunate to have experience in successfully building social networks from the ground up. The first step in building your network is to identify the who. It's not a numbers game, as many people will lead you to believe. When it comes to community building, I preach three simple words: *quality over quantity*. You want the *right* people on your page, not the most. The right audience leads to engagement. Engagement leads to sales—or in your case enrollment, packed stadiums, and successful recruiting classes. You want your community to be engaged on their own, whether you are there or not.

A surefire way to lose engagement is to stockpile fans who couldn't care less about what you're talking about and derail conversations rather than contribute to them. If I'm a fan of Virginia Tech soccer, I want to talk about Virginia Tech soccer, not Virginia Tech tennis, not politics, and I definitely don't want to have to debate with my cross-town rivals every time I log on. It's easier to lose fans than it is to keep them. The more you can fill your community with like-minded individuals, the more likely you are to maintain a viable community. Quality over quantity: words to build communities by.

social networks are like snowflakes

It's important to manage and treat each social platform differently, as each is built for different forms of engagement. Facebook is different from Twitter, Twitter from Instagram, and so on and so on. Brian Reich and Dan Solomon said as much in their book *Media Rules!*, telling readers to "understand why and how your audience uses technology and then start trying to align your communication efforts" (2007). Makes sense, but because of a lack of time and resources, brands often push the exact same content on all managed social platforms. The problem is, if I'm a fan of your brand, I'm likely following you on both Facebook and Twitter with the expectation that each will deliver unique content and experiences. According to a study conducted by the Pew Research Center, 42 percent of adults online use multiple social networking platforms (2013). If you deliver me the same content in both spaces, I have no reason to follow you on more than one platform. At that point the brand loses a point of contact with the consumer. That's a miss. Leverage and treat each platform differently and watch them thrive.

42%

42 percent of adults online use multiple social networking platforms.

During my time at adidas, we looked at how each social space could be leveraged to our advantage. By 2013, Facebook numbers in terms of users were still strong; however, engagement among our high school athlete demographic had changed. So we did too. Facebook more than any other social channel allowed for deeper conversations, much like a dot-com, while other channels like Twitter had character limits, which prevented us from diving into product benefits.

As a result, we started to treat Facebook as an extension of our football and baseball online homes (adidasfootball.com and adidasbaseball.com). These were places where kids could come to find out in greater detail what separated our products from the competition.

We chose to treat Twitter in a different way entirely. For me, Twitter has always been social networking's version of reality TV. It's easier to leverage a platform's competencies than try to change them. Rather than attempting to establish a product voice that didn't seem to fit the medium, we chose to let our athletes and partners speak on our behalf, with our own channel being used for in-the-moment conversations (let's talk about what's happening right now versus talking about what happened yesterday). By using our athletes as spokespeople and only speaking as a brand when relevant conversation existed, we found a genuine and authentic way to insert our voice into the space.

Instagram was different still. "Insta" became the place where the culture and personality of adidas Football came to life. This was not where you would find information on the traction or stability of our cleats, but you would find photos capturing the in-between and candid moments around our athletes and partners or a behind-the-scenes look at a surprise concert we threw for the athletes participating in the US Army All-American Bowl. Instragram became the platform that gave us, as a football brand, a soul.

Three social networks, each used in a unique way that was genuine to the user and platform while still benefiting our brand and effectively telling our story. There will likely never again be just one online social space. You will always be challenged to balance multiple platforms. Beyond Facebook, Twitter, and Instagram, there will be others like Tumblr, Vine, and Snapchat that come along. How you embrace the differences of each will determine how successful you are at driving branded conversations online.

> ❝ understand why and how your audience uses technology and then start trying to align your communication efforts. ❞ (brian reich and dan solomon)

week one or bust

Social media is nothing more than a series of algorithms and patterns waiting to be cracked. I found that out firsthand in my time managing the Robert Griffin III (RGIII) brand at adidas. September 9, 2013, would be a big day for a lot of people and organizations. It would be an important day for adidas, the NFL, my colleagues, and me. And most important, it would be a big day for Robert Griffin III. That would be the day RGIII would return from recovering from a major knee injury suffered at the end of the previous season, his rookie year, to play in week one of the 2013 campaign. There had been a tremendous amount of hype and debate around Griffin's return. Adidas played a part in the ongoing storyline, having built a TV campaign supporting Griffin's rehabilitation from the devastating injury. The campaign's motto was "all in for week 1," a phrase that aligned with the brand's mantra and one that would be uttered countless times by the media leading up to the game and throughout the off-season. It was that phrase that would ignite a firestorm of debate around whether or not Griffin should return for the first week of the season.

By the middle of August, all signs pointed to Griffin playing. As the sports performance brand sponsoring RGIII, we knew it was our responsibility and our pleasure to support him. Our mantra around the former Heisman Trophy winner and NFL Offensive Rookie of the Year turned from supporting the journey to supporting the accomplishment. A tremendous amount of work, at a level I will never be able to fully understand, paid off. Griffin was ready to take the field. The opening week game was against the Philadelphia Eagles on *Monday Night Football*, the most anticipated game of the season's first weekend. Our goal was to show RGIII and the rest of the country that he was part of our family and that we were proud to call him #teamadidas.

It was that hashtag (#teamadidas) that would become the mantra and unifier for the campaign and the avenue from which we would show him our support. It became our mission to get #teamadidas to trend on Twitter during the much-talked-about matchup between two fierce NFC East rivals.

We rallied everyone in our network to tweet a good luck message to @RGIII just before the game, at the same exact time, to the minute. From friends and family to all of our agency partners, from athletes like former NBA Rookie of the Year Damian Lillard of the Portland Trail Blazers to our celebrity endorsers like Snoop Dogg; everyone tweeted at the same moment, including the hashtag #teamadidas.

The results were amazing. The hashtag #teamadidas trended three times during the first part of a game that became the most viewed week one game since ESPN started broadcasting games in 2006 and the number one telecast that night across all channels. All eyes were on this game, and those following along via Twitter saw our support of beloved partner RGIII and the strength of our brand's bond. Our Twitter engagement was up 100 percent, with *#teamadidas* being the phrase most associated with *RGIII* online. At the end of the night, adidas Football's overall sentiment (as measured via conversation online) was up 2 percent.

The lesson here is that a coordinated approach on social networking can elicit results without major media dollars. Pick a key moment, leverage your current and former players or coaches, rally your student body, involve the surrounding community and town—anyone and everyone you can find to support your effort—and you will see similar results.

tweets at the ready

Sporting events are a hotbed for social media engagement, and Twitter has become the preferred platform for users across the world to digitally join the conversation in real-time. During game seven of the NBA Finals between the Miami Heat and the San Antonio Spurs, over 7.3 million game-related tweets were sent by 1.9 million unique authors (Nielsen, February 4, 2014). Brand and digital marketing managers everywhere are trying to find ways to capitalize. Aptly calling this approach "real-time marketing," brands are using it to insert themselves into the conversation with hyper-focused and relevant digital content, product placement, messaging, and more.

The potential return on investment around real-time marketing is tremendous. That's because in many cases it costs nothing while returning millions of dollars in brand exposure.

Take the 2014 Grammys, for example. At the event, hip-hop artist Pharrell Williams stole the show thanks to his abnormally large and equally odd hat, which happened to resemble the Arby's logo. The fast food chain's social media manager, Josh Martin, was following the event and conversation, as any great social media manager should. Seeing an opportunity to react, he tweeted at Pharrell with a simple message that snowballed into the company's biggest social media response ever. Martin simply tweeted: "Hey @Pharrell can we have our hat back? #Grammys."

The results were staggering: over 83,000 retweets, 48,000 favorites, 10,700 replies, and 6,000 new followers (Gesenhues, January 29, 2014). According to Martin, that single sentence earned 384 times more reach than the brand's average. Pharrell himself got involved by responding to the brand's tweet by asking, "Ya'll tryna start a roast beef?"

Be ready; your time will come.

83,000	48,000	10,700	6,000
RETWEETS	FAVORITES	REPLIES	NEW FOLLOWERS

keep the cape, superman

In January of 2014, I was flying home from the US Army All-American Game, an event adidas Football sponsored, and one I was in charge of from a brand and digital marketing perspective. It was during the flight home that an idea struck me. For the game, we had hired a pair of artists to person-alize each athlete's cleat with a saying, nickname, or design of the player's choice. Incredibly, in forty-eight hours, the artists were able to customize over 120 cleats. The turnaround time for such beautifully designed detail blew me away and inspired me.

The following week adidas athlete Frank Gore and the San Francisco 49ers would take on Cam Newton and the Carolina Panthers in the second round of the NFL Playoffs. During the regular season, Newton, an Under Armour athlete, routinely stepped onto the field in Superman-themed cleats during pregame warm-ups. And every Sunday, like clockwork, the media ate it up.

It was too easy to pass up. We had a Pro Bowl athlete in Frank Gore on the opposing team, a signature cleat in adizero that was the antithesis of Newton's Highlight cleat from Under Armour, and we had Superman's only weakness: kryptonite. Or at least we would.

When I landed back home in Portland, I got on the phone with one of the artists from the US Army game and asked how quickly he could turn an all-white adizero into the football cleat version of kryptonite.

Within forty-eight hours, we had in our possession a cleat designed to resemble the green crystals from the planet Krypton that routinely foiled Su-perman, executed a photo shoot, and built creative to launch on gameday.

Now we just needed the story to play out on the field. Lucky for us, it did. Late in the game, with the 49ers up on the road, our boy Frank Gore broke free for a long run that led to the final score of the game. We had our moment.

With only a couple of minutes left and the 49ers all but assured of the win, we pushed out a photo of our custom adizero lying on top of a bed of kryptonite. The accompanying copy read: "Keep the cape, we have adizero. #frankgore #adizero." The tone was dripping with confidence and bravado.

It would go on to become one of the most engaging social posts of our year. Our fans loved it. The formula was clear. Provocative messaging in real-time, with relevant content, leads to success. "I'm continually amazed at fans' level of engagement with sports content—it's like they can't get enough," said Stephen Master, senior vice president of sports, Nielsen. "Regardless of what device or screen consumers use to access it, sports remains one of the most captivating genres of programming and is well-positioned to thrive in this increasingly fragmented media marketplace" (Nielsen, February 13, 2014).

don't beat 'em, join 'em

You'll never be able to control message boards, as many of them are managed by and overrun by bleeding-heart subscribers. But, if you can't beat 'em, join 'em! Message boards can be your best friend then. Think of them as free market research. Befriend the admins of the boards you consider to be the most relevant in your community and partner with them. The reason is simple: you're catering to fans, and fans are the lifeblood of your program. The more you know about them, the more likely you are to keep them happy. Message boards offer you free focus groups and a finger on the pulse of your fan base at any given moment. All you have to do is plug in that URL and start reading.

Consider this: if you're looking to gauge fan response to a new, unreleased uniform idea, your friends the forum admins can test the waters for you without giving away the farm. And they'll do it just in time for you to react and tweak designs.

Similarly, if you have a new brand campaign you're trying to make headway with among fans, create message board signatures (the banners you often see underneath posts of particular individuals) that the admins can offer up to their community exclusively. In a matter of days, your new campaign will be all over the internet, thanks to your decision to seed the art to your most rabid fan base.

I know this can work because, as a die-hard Oregon State University fan and alum, I once volunteered my time with a noteworthy Beavers board and created school-specific signatures for the community. The response was great, and still to this day I see posts that include a signature I designed.

Message boards are your friends, not your foes, as many would assume. These boards are a resource to you. Market research is expensive; message boards are free. Use them.

when the fire starts to die, buy more wood

There is only so much conversation that you can "earn." Sometimes you need to simply open up your wallet and pay your way into households through bought media. The key is choosing the platform that works best for the moment and fitting your story into that space, rather than the other way around.

money *can* buy you love

Here's a tip for those of you looking to build strong social communities through paid media: invest in pay-per-engagement (also known as cost-per-engagement, CPE) models in which you pay only when a user takes an action; meaning the user likes, shares, or comments on your content, among other things. By doing so, you begin to build your communities with the right individuals. The best thing about social networks is the ability to target. If you want to talk to high school wrestlers in North Dakota, you can. CPE models cut out the waste you get from buying on a cost-per-impression (CPM) basis, which will have you paying each time your ad is "served" (at a rate of 1,000) or displayed (also known as an impression). No matter the audience seeing your ad, you pay for that impression, which is a much less controllable situation. Also, impressions can be a hollow metric. Your ad may garner one million impressions, but if only 5 percent of those impressions come from your preferred target, does it make sense? Was it effective? It depends on the goal. With the impression model, you do "waste" money on those outside your target market who happen upon your ad.

YouTube offers effective CPE models that allow you to buy preroll ads (ads that run prior to the video a user intends to watch) that only draw from your budget if a certain number of seconds are seen by the user. More important that preroll view contributes to your video's total view count on YouTube. Why is that important? Because the more views you get on your video, the more likely that video is to show up naturally when people search anything related to it, giving you residual, organic, and free views down the road.

Cost-per-click (CPC), another engagement-driven program, is also cost effective because you pay only when someone actually clicks on your ad or likes your page. In the case of Facebook, that's a win-win. Another big company that sells CPC ads is Google. You can buy search terms through Google on a CPC basis. So for instance, if you have a Heisman campaign running, buying the term *Heisman* would be an effective spend to support your campaign (although you have to realize you're likely not the only one bidding on that term, which drives up costs).

Now let's connect the dots. Once a user finds your Heisman campaign through search, you can then drive that potential click-through to one of the previously mentioned social platforms of your choice. Upon arrival, that user should find a Heisman hype video lauding your candidate, which is pulling directly from your YouTube account. This means that every visit to your social network, which is driven in part by traffic from your search campaign, is also a potential view of your YouTube video. At that point you have effectively closed the loop by connecting search, social, and video in one seamless campaign.

As I've said, social networking is a puzzle based on algorithms. What I have learned is that the more you work with these channels, the more ways you discover how to manipulate each, leading to a self-sustaining social ecosystem that feeds off itself whether you're there to water it or not.

The above examples are not meant to promote Facebook, Google, or YouTube. Those are all very effective channels to advertise on, no doubt; however, the point of the above is to give you examples of how to take advantage of these big networks and how to effectively advertise in today's world. By the time you read this, there will likely be a new media-buying model and network infiltrating the digital space, but if I'm doing my job right, these philosophies will not change, regardless of the platform. Social media marketing expenditure in the United States is expected to reach $5 billion by 2016 (Statista.com, 2014). Be smart with how you spend your money; ensure every ad bought increases the size of the pool of individuals you have to speak with when the next opportunity arises.

$5 billion

social media marketing expenditure in the united states is expected to reach $5 billion by 2016.

it's 3:00 a.m.; do you know where your media is running?

If visuals are key to your communication plan (for instance, if you're promoting a new uniform), digital display banners are, of course, an option. However, be wary of falling victim to the "run of network/site" sales pitches that you will no doubt get from vendors. Run of network media buying means buying advertising from a company that owns several sites—without the ability to choose which sites your media runs on. Run of site is a similar idea, with the difference being that rather than running your media among a series of sites, you run your media throughout a single site. The problem is, in each case, you have no idea where your ads will run or when, which has never made any sense to me. The vendor is merely selling the client on cost efficiencies. When brands don't have major media budgets, run of network buys sound pretty good. However, to me it's just a wasted spend. I would much rather put my money into the social space through CPC ads and complement that spend with the highest impact banner placement I can afford, to make a splash. As a consumer, I'm more likely to remember a visually compelling page takeover on a site I frequent than I am a standard media banner at the bottom right of a page I happen to be reading an article on. Once again, I'm all about quality over quantity.

go to print

One of the tried-and-true forms of advertising, print advertising, can be a great awareness driver, and it happens to be one of the most trusted. Over 60 percent of North Americans trust newspaper and magazine ads, ranking number one and two respectively among all forms of advertising (Statista .com, 2014). When you are debating print, you must first determine what scale of audience you're looking to target. If it's local, and you're simply trying to fill seats, your hometown or state papers and magazines will do the job. If it's national, and you're looking to drive broader awareness around your program, you really need to start looking at wider-reaching publications.

60%
over 60 percent of north americans trust newspaper and magazine ads.

The other thing to consider here is frequency. How many consecutive insertions (the number of consecutive issues your ad appears in) can you afford in a given publication? My own personal rule is a minimum of three. If I can't afford to be in three consecutive issues, print isn't in the cards for me. That's because I've learned and believe it takes at minimum three views of an ad for it to stick with the audience.

The last thing I'll say about print is that if you're going to use it, you better be doing something that stands out. That means telling a unique and compelling story. Build around a culture moment, such as a highly anticipated game or new uniform launch—things that you know will elicit emotion from your audience. Make sure your creative jumps off the page, stands out, and gets people talking!

I've had the good fortune of working on some pretty amazing projects in my time at adidas. The print example that stands out is the story we manufactured for the 2013 NFL Scouting Combine. For years we had the lightest cleat in football, and many of the elite high school players knew about it. It was a story that struck a chord. But at that point, every football brand was pushing speed. The truth of the matter was, only the brand with the lightest cleat could truly substantiate the claim of being the fastest. That was us. But we needed to make it known to the masses, not just the elite talent. We needed to disrupt. The Combine was our platform. On the day the first group of skill players ran the 40-yard dash, we wrapped the cover of the *Indianapolis Star* (the paper of record where the Combine was held and where all key media, players, and agents were staying) with an ad that simply read, *Run the fastest 40, get a contract offer—adidas Football*. It was a simple, easy-to-read ad that had two things going for it: the creative jumped off the page and caught your attention from newsstands using big and bold lettering that could be read from a distance, and the story itself was unique and dripping with swagger. No brand had ever made such an offer; it made people stop and say, "Holy cow, look at what adidas did." We spent very little money on the idea, but it was such a compelling story, and it executed so well on the cover of the *Star* that ESPN ran the story on its home page, traditionally a space reserved for sport-specific stories, not brand integrations. Adidas Football had never achieved that level of coverage from the nation's top sports news source. The project was deemed a tremendous success and only furthered our association with speed and lightweight foot-wear. As is the case with any medium, do something unexpected or run the risk of blending in.

do something unexpected or run the risk of blending in.

back from the dead

Radio is unlikely to make or break a campaign; however, what radio can be is another point of frequency. Remember that the keys to making an idea stick are consistency and frequency. Radio can give you another hammer to the nail that is your brand story. The more times you hit the nail, the further it goes in—and the harder it is to get out.

Some of you might be reading this and saying to yourselves, "Radio is dead." And at some level, when speaking of traditional radio, part of me agrees with you. But only part. According to a 2014 Nielsen report, each week, radio reaches over 91 percent of Americans aged twelve and up. That means 242 million people are listening to the radio on a weekly basis. I wouldn't write radio off just yet. Radio is not like it used to be. No longer are you limited to AM/FM stations. Today we have digital services like Pandora, Spotify, and iTunes Radio, where kids and adults both are flocking to stream their favorite music. Radio isn't dead. It's evolving.

242M

242 million people are listening to the radio
on a weekly basis.

The benefit of buying media in these digital radio spaces is that not only
do you get the traditional audio ad but now you also get digital banner
space along with it. But what if you didn't stop there? What if you leveraged
what inherently makes audio so prevalent even today? What if you made
your own music? Digital radio stations provide a fantastic launching pad for
new music, which any school can take advantage of.

In January 2013, Notre Dame's football team was on its way to playing Alabama in the national championship. With that came a tremendous
opportunity for both Notre Dame and adidas to bring attention to and build
hype around the storied program. The challenge was in finding something
that would resonate with high school athletes, every football program's
target market. We turned to music. Music plays a major role in football
culture. From the gym to the locker room to the field, music is in the DNA of
all sports. And Notre Dame has one of the most recognizable fight songs in
all of college athletics, which gave us a terrific canvas to work with. We used
it to generate excitement around the program prior to the game, partner-
ing with a prominent DJ to remix the fight song and seed it out through
music and culture media outlets like Complex. The result was national PR
coverage that helped lead to over one million streams of the song prior to
the game.

Music transcends all age groups, all demographics, all sports. It's a
medium that is underutilized by schools today but is one that can be very
effective.

brands **defenses win championships**

hey, macklemore, can we go thrift shopping?

In 2012, I led a team responsible for launching a series of new uniforms around our top adidas NCAA football programs. As part of that launch, I worked with our agency partner in Portland, Roundhouse, to develop video content to go out with each press announcement. As usual, the Roundhouse team came up with a concept I loved and one that tied seamlessly back to the brand tone we developed together for the year.

Leaning on my own experience as a fan, I was looking for content that felt more reminiscent of a music video, showcasing our beautiful uniform designs in a way that got people out of their chairs, versus speaking to the science and technology behind each creation. I wanted what the high school athlete was asking for. And we got it. Almost.

We still needed music. Whether it be for TV or for YouTube, I've always put emphasis on song selection. In my experience, a melody can make or break your work. A TV spot or digital video with the wrong music is like pairing a $10,000 suit with $5 sandals. The suit is ruined, and so is the video.

a TV spot or digital video with the wrong music is like pairing a $10,000 suit with $5 sandals.

In this particular instance, I was less worried about the name of the artist and more concerned about the sound. Did the song itself fit the tone we were trying to capture? Did it get me out of my chair, ready to put the pads on and hit someone?

Fortunately, after weeks of listening to potential tracks submitted to us by several music studios, we found it. Hidden between song after song was "Can't Hold Us," a title from a then little-known duo out of Seattle by the name of Macklemore & Ryan Lewis. It was perfect. The beat, the hook, the message: it all worked, and our community loved it. Over the years the content I've worked on has consistently drawn as much praise for the music as the video itself. Music is the perfect way to bring in the ever-elusive cultural currency all of us marketers, and the brands we work for, seek.

What I didn't realize when we picked that song is that the little-known duo from the Pacific Northwest would go on to release two singles less than a year later that would reach number one on the US Billboard Hot 100 Chart. One of those singles was "Can't Hold Us."

air their dirty laundry

For a while it seemed brand managers and media agencies were done with out of home (OOH) advertising, such as billboards and wallscapes, but I have a sneaking suspicion it's on its way back, and it's one of the advertising placements I get most excited about. Outdoor advertising can become a nice complement to the bigger media mix campaign you have running. With OOH you have an opportunity to get creative and truly be disruptive. Take advantage of the canvas you have. Be extraordinary. Be unexpected. Be buzzworthy. Use the outdoors to get people talking.

be extraordinary.
be unexpected.
be buzzworthy.

Look back at what the University of Oregon did during the Joey Harrington Heisman campaign. The billboard the school purchased in Manhattan wasn't based on the number of on-the-ground impressions it would get. No, the reason the school bought the billboard was for the PR and buzz it would ultimately generate around their top player and their team—nationally. Your school might not be able to afford a billboard in New York City, but you can still take the same disruptive approach to your outdoor media buying.

A favorite tactic of mine is buying branded billboard space in the hometown of a rival school. Chances are, depending on the scale of your rivalry, the simple purchase and production of that space is going to get covered by media. Imagine an Ohio State billboard going up in Ann Arbor, Michigan, or a Louisville Cardinals billboard going up in Lexington, Kentucky. The media love rivalries. Be provocative. Stir the pot. Create controversy. A scandalous billboard in your rival's backyard is media gold and sure to create conversation. Remember that sexy rivalries are good for your brand and good for business.

Finally, because many of the top athletic institutions in the country reside in small towns (Tuscaloosa, Alabama; Baton Rouge, Louisiana; Ann Arbor, Michigan) where populations do not warrant high media costs, OOH becomes an affordable way to bring attention to your program. This is a medium that can produce a great return on your investment if executed in an effective way.

it's good to be king

According to a 2014 AdWeek study conducted with ad targeting firm Simul-media, there are 283 million television viewers each month (the population of the United States is 313 million), each watching an average of 146 hours of TV. Compare that with 155 million online video viewers averaging just shy of six hours monthly on mobile and almost six and a half hours over the web. TV is still the media king.

And while TV may be the most effective perception driver of all media platforms, with that reward comes considerable risk. TV is expensive, and it's not worth the money unless you have something compelling to say and the audience to say it to. Plus, timing is crucial. It doesn't make a ton of sense to me to invest exclusively in TV ads running during games featuring your program and thus likely only being watched by existing fans. Unless it's a culture moment, you're not talking to anyone new, so why spend all of your money there?

If you're going to invest in TV, save your money to advertise during a nationally televised and nationally relevant game. In fact, consider promoting your team during your rival's game, even if you're not the opposing team. In that case you're likely still talking to many of your own fans (let's face it, we all watch our rival's games hoping beyond hope that the team loses) while at the same time talking to a great number of potential fans. Plus, like our out of home example, the simple fact that you bought media space during your rival's game is a story in and of itself that will get people talking, including the media, pouring more gasoline onto the rivalry flame.

As in any media campaign, be disruptive. If you're going to invest in TV, invest in strong creative and wait until you have something meaningful to say along with a meaningful moment to say it.

get aggressive!
get people
talking!

Imagine ESPN or Fox chooses your rivalry for its "game of the week," a moment in which a national TV audience that reaches well beyond your traditional fan base will be watching. These are the types of moments brand marketers dream of. These are the moments to take your most relevant and compelling topic and bring it to life. What better time or place to run an ad promoting your very own National Player of the Year candidate? Or maybe your team won this particular rivalry game the previous year. Why not build an ad that specifically highlights that victory? Poor some salt into that wound! Get aggressive! Get people talking! That is exactly the type of provocative message that stirs the pot. Show some swagger! High school athletes will love you for it.

Here's the other reality that should be taken very seriously: quality TV production is expensive. Building a brand is expensive. But you get what you pay for. How many low-budget university ads have you seen during televised college sporting events? Too many to count. How many Apple- or Gatorade-level university ads have you seen? Zero. That is what gets me fired up. The door is wide open. The opportunity is right in front of every school in the country. Invest in your brand to build your brand.

what's on second screen?

Today mobile marketing is a fixture in the overall media mix, with research suggesting that global mobile ad spending will reach nearly $40 billion by 2018 (Rolands, October 22, 2013). That means the days of simply resizing your desktop ads to fit the smaller mobile screen are over. The consumption experience on a phone or tablet is completely different from that of a computer, and because of that, it requires a media approach that services its own unique needs. Build your ads to leverage the environment and scenarios that can only be found on a mobile device.

Our adidas Football team did just that at the 2014 NFL Scouting Combine. The previous year, in which we caught everyone off guard by offering a contract to the player who ran the fastest 40, was just the beginning. Much to the chagrin of our competition, we upped the ante in '14, this time giving $100,000 to the player with the quickest 40-yard dash in our newest adizero cleat.

Once again all eyes and all conversation were focused squarely on the brand with three stripes, and this time we would lean heavily on mobile media to elevate the story. While print continued to be a key piece of the puzzle, it was our collective effort around mobile that allowed us to be the most talked about sporting goods brand on Twitter during the Combine. That was a feat in and of itself, considering it was our competition that sponsored the Combine and the NFL.

At every key moment, we were ready with mobile support, knowing that the majority of engagement around the Combine and our story would come via Twitter—specifically by way of phones or tablets. On the day we announced our cash offer, we bought the mobile takeover of ESPN.com's NFL home page, complemented by a Twitter ad in which we promoted tweets made by our key athletes. By doing so, we allowed the message to reach a much broader audience, while coming from a voice that our high school target respected and trusted.

It was the Twitter buy that would ultimately lead to our success. While the audacity of the offer was crucial in putting the spotlight on our brand from the outset, it was our mobile-driven Twitter activity that carried the conversation throughout the week, allowing us to sustain buzz and peak during key moments.

Those moments included appearances by Snoop Dogg, as well as newly signed adidas athlete and former Clemson All-American Sammy Watkins, to our product suite. It was there that athletes competing at the Combine would receive their adidas cleats to wear in the forthcoming events. Both the Snoop Dogg and the Sammy Watkins appearances were followed by tweets and product endorsements from each icon that we then pushed out to a larger audience through paid media. Everything worked together seamlessly.

The combination of versatile social media spending allowed us to react to both anticipated and unanticipated moments, along with delivering those stories to the consumers on the mobile devices on which they would ultimately engage, directly contributing to the tremendous buzz surrounding the campaign.

The 2014 NFL Scouting Combine will go down as one of the proudest moments I will ever have as a brand marketer and professional. We were David battling Goliath in this case, and it was a collective effort and flawless execution by a group of passionate and driven individuals that brought us such success. And it was that collective effort and execution that ultimately resulted in an on-air mention during a prime-time episode of ESPN's SportsCenter the week of the Combine, the holy grail of press coverage in our industry. Great things can happen when you align all of your channels and key partners in telling one consistent story.

this for that

One thing that goes very much underutilized in the media world is bartering. This is a tactic I've used consistently over my career, specifically with media and retail partners. Content is king, and you have valuable content to offer: players and coaches. Barter with media outlets who target the demographic you want to talk with by offering up inside access to your program in return for space on their sites or in their magazines (i.e., free media and exposure).

If a vendor wants access to our adidas Football and Baseball athletes or coaches, the first question I ask is, "What's in it for us?" Bartering can be a great way to earn media when you don't have media money. If you've found a taker, go one step further and create an ongoing program with the site so that you can brand the way you want to brand. If you're the University of Tennessee and you have a Naismith Award candidate at center, create a program along with a relevant outlet in which your center blogs once a week exclusively on their site. Brand the blog in a way that tells your story while at the same time getting the word out on your award candidate. Never accept the initial offer; always look to take it to the next level and tell your brand story.

experience of a lifetime

You need money to make money, and much of that money comes from selling out your home games and hosted events. The problem is that there are very few stadium, arena, or ballpark experiences that stand out these days. If your school is among those falling into the mundane category, then your fans are likely only coming to see you during the good times. That is not a sustainable business model. Your goal should be to create such an overwhelmingly enjoyable experience (*experience* is the key word here) that fans come out in droves, win or lose. Let's get to it and talk about how to take your in-stadium experience from mundane to something people will be compelled to talk about and write about.

gators, bulldogs, and cocktails

What's one of the first things you see when you arrive on an SEC campus during Saturdays in the fall? Tailgating. A *lot* of tailgating. And you better believe it contributes to the general perception that the teams in the Southeastern Conference have the best football fans in America. The game experience starts and finishes in the parking lots just outside the stadium. You want to create a name for your school, your town, your team? Get your fans to tailgate. You want to bring in new fans? Get your fans to tailgate. You want to fill your stadium? Get your fans to tailgate. Make it a party, and people will come in bunches, win or lose.

ESPN routinely covers the best tailgating experiences. One such experience comes from the annual Florida vs. Georgia football game held in Jacksonville, Florida, in which, it can be argued, the tailgating is more well-known than the game itself. Since the 1950s, the tailgating experience prior

make it a party, and people will come in bunches, win or lose.

to the game has been called the World's Largest Outdoor Cocktail Party. Media love to report from and engage with hometown tailgates like these at every school they visit, which makes it an even more important piece of your gameday experience. The better the tailgating experience and the more rabid your fans seem, the stronger your program feels. The Mississippi State Bulldogs baseball program has taken this approach to the next level still by integrating tailgating into the actual in-game experience. Dubbed the Left Field Lounge, the best seats in the house are located in the outfield and aren't seats in the traditional sense at all. Instead of bleachers you'll find pickup trucks, RVs, motor homes, and trailers, many equipped with barbeques and all the finest tailgating amenities.

"What began in the 1960s as a popular gathering spot for baseball loving MSU students now forms college baseball's largest tailgating party," says Hailstate.com, Mississippi State's sports site. The gameday experience became so popular that *Sports Illustrated* called watching a game from the Left Field Lounge one of the "100 things you gotta do before you graduate" (2003). Like everything else, tailgating needs your support to be effective. Don't discourage your fans—encourage them!

fill your stands!

This is a subject that has always felt like low-hanging fruit to me, yet so often I find myself watching games on TV with empty stadiums and arenas. I don't get it. Let's go back to the previous restaurant example and connect it directly to the in-stadium experience. Stadiums (or ballparks or fields, etc.) are a lot like restaurants in that perception is reality. Empty restaurants are often perceived to have bad food, poor service, or something that is generally keeping people away. Given the choice of an empty restaurant or a restaurant with a line out the door, most people are going to hold out for the more popular option, assuming the food must be great, given the apparent popularity.

Stadiums can be viewed the same way. Empty stadiums are assumed to house a bad team and a lame experience; why would anyone want to go? It surprises me how many universities allow their teams to play on regional or (gasp!) national television with less than full stadiums or arenas. Fill your stands! If you can't sell your tickets, give them away. You're not going to sell those tickets anyway, so rather than turning fans or recruits off by your sparsely attended event, create the perception that you have the hottest ticket in town. Do that, and slowly but surely your seats should start to fill themselves with warm, paying bodies.

Speaking of giving tickets away, who better to give away tickets to than potential fans? Even better, how about potential fans who might one day become potential recruits? If you can't fill your stadium with paying fans, find a local high school and give the tickets to that school. Invite them as your guests and make sure every attendee from that school gets a free shirt. That shirt and your brand will suddenly start showing up all over the halls of your most fertile recruiting ground: high schools.

if you can't sell
your tickets,
give them away.

Whether you are able to sell out your stadium regularly or not, I'd suggest developing an ongoing ticket-giveaway program that works on a rotational basis with local schools in your community and state. It's a long-term strategy to sustain and grow your fan base. Work now to win the hearts and minds of the next generation of local fans and athletes.

make an entrance

Traditions can be born out of the simplest things—even things like entrance music. Virginia Tech football and its "Enter Sandman," by Metallica, entrance is a great example. I love what the Hokies have done. By being consistent with its entrance music, the school has created a tradition. There are few stadiums that get as loud as Lane Stadium before the hometown Hokies run onto the field to one of the most recognizable heavy metal songs of all time. Music selection has a lot to do with that.

My suggestion to you and your school would be to find a song with similar energy to play before your team leaves the tunnel—but take it one step further. Find a song that not only has energy but also contributes to your brand story. I'm not sure what "Enter Sandman" has to do with Virginia Tech; it may have a deeper meaning than I am aware of. However, if it doesn't, there is a brand-building opportunity being left on the table. Remember that *everything* you do should contribute to building your identity. Find a song with energy, find a song with meaning, and start building that tradition.

everything **you do should contribute to building your identity.**

gear me

When it comes to gameday fan gear, two basketball programs come to mind: Cal and Duke. Both distinguished student bodies are known for wearing their striped polos to basketball games, and I love it. It's such a simple tradition, and it ties directly to the positioning of each school—scholarly institutions rooted in the polo-wearing upper crust of society. Some might call it snobbery; I call it branding.

When looking at starting your own gameday apparel tradition, start with your story and use your student ambassadors to write your future. Let your students become physical manifestations of who your university and athletic program are. If you're an aggie school, get your students in overalls. If you're an Ivy League school, get your student section in shirts and ties. If you're a blue-collar program, get your students in hard hats! Find what makes your program unique, dress up the student body, and *own* it!

Don't forget color. When I think of fan gear on gameday, I think about the experience, and that experience for me starts with a sea of color. Like we talked about earlier in this book, it's important as a collegiate brand to own a color. When you do decide what color that is, make sure that's the shade you blanket your bookstore with. It's your job to ensure every fan rolling through your town on gameday leaves the bookstore with that color on his or her back.

well, paint my face red

What do you think of when you hear "face-painting stations"? Kids, right? I'll tell you what I think of: eighteen-to-twenty-two-year-old college students full of energy, passion, and maybe a little alcohol. You've got to get into the weeds to affect perception. Yes, I said "into," not "out of." The little things can sometimes be more important than the big. Your objective is to create an experience that fans and recruits never forget, and fanatics can go a long way in making that experience memorable and fun. When you see hundreds of students with their bodies and faces painted in their school's colors, it makes an impact. And as a fan or recruit, you're going to walk away thinking that particular town is crazy about their team. I don't care who you are, that's attractive. Create a Comic-Con–like atmosphere. Make it easy for your fans to become fanatics, give them the tools, and watch as your stadium experience goes from good to great.

hooligans

The first American school to replicate the experience of an English Premier League (EPL) soccer match has itself an atmosphere unlike any other in college sports. The EPL does it right, and college sports are ripe to emulate those packed stadiums in England. Throughout the full ninety minutes of an EPL match, you'll hear the entire stadium rotating through a variety of cheers, chants, and songs, all supporting a team or degrading the rival squad. It's an electricity no college stadium or arena has yet to match, which means there is a major opportunity out there for a school to create such an experience and get credit for it nationally.

the first american school to replicate the experience of an epl soccer match has an atmosphere unlike any other in college sports.

Imagine the impact you can have on a group of recruits visiting your stadium, welcomed by over fifty thousand rabid fans chanting the same thing in unison. You have very little time to make an impression on a young man or woman visiting your campus on a recruiting trip; it's scenes like these that can make or break a commitment to your program.

From my own history, the closest thing to an EPL stadium experience in college sports is when the entire Wisconsin Badgers student section jumps up and down and sings "Jump Around," by House of Pain, between the third and fourth quarters of home football games. It's an experience like nothing I've seen in sports. The problem is that it happens when no one is on the field, so the impact on the game is minimal. Plus, it's very brief and the only moment of its kind during the game. There's no other significant chant or cheer that follows.

I would be doing a disservice to the school if I didn't also mention Texas A&M and its in-game traditions, all choreographed beautifully and practiced each night before home games by the faithful student body. Wisconsin and Texas A&M represent two of the better in-game executions in the country, but there is plenty of room to grow.

Now, you knew this was coming: when orchestrating your cheers and chants, start with the brand story and work from there. Your cheers should stay in line with your position as a brand and contribute to telling that story. If it were me, this would be one of the first places I invested my time.

mascots need love too

Mascots have become media darlings in the last few years. Between Capitol One's Mascot Challenge and ESPN's consistent use of mascots in their commercials, these characters are more relevant than ever. If you don't have a mascot, get one. If you're not in the Mascot Challenge, find a way in. If you haven't sent your mascot's uniform to ESPN's studios, do it now. This a great way to get your brand out in front of people. Another hammer to the nail. Don't underestimate anything at your disposal. Pull every lever you have to keep your brand top of mind.

When it comes to the appearance and presentation of your mascot, go back to your brand story. Your mascot becomes a walking and talking version of your story. There are very few areas where you can be more transparent about who you are as a program than through your mascot. Mascots have no shame—that's the point.

Similarly, your mascot's actions speak just as loud as his or her appearance. Mascots have a license to do just about anything during a game, which opens the door for you to choreograph activities and stunts that further establish who you are as a program. Think very carefully about how your mascot represents you, and use those moments to help solidify your identity.

get the band back together

Just like your mascot, your band is a walking, talking, and music-playing representation of who you are and want to be as a program. Be mindful of the uniforms; use that space to tell your story. Be aware of the playlist; use those music notes to tell your story. Get involved in deciding what routines the band performs and when; use the choreography to tell your story. You get the picture: bands can help you get where you want to go.

two burgers, one fry, and a brand story to go

If you have the opportunity to affect the names of the restaurants in your stadium and the products they're selling, use them to tell your story. If your program is all about flash, give the establishments and their products names that elevate that idea. If your program is all about being blue-collar, then keep the names within that theme. Have every fan walking around with lunch pails of food and thermoses for their drinks. Have fun with it! It might sound cheesy, but it works. Remember, it's an experience for these fans and families attending. Every single opportunity to reinforce your message is crucial. Don't let even the smallest opportunity slip by without your affecting it. According to the *Ann Arbor News*, during a typical University of Michigan football game, concessionaires will sell an average of 65,000 bottles of water (November 17, 2012). That's 455,000 bottles of water sold during a season of seven home games. Imagine the penetration your story could have if it were being told on the wrappers covering those bottles of water.

65,000
during a typical University of Michigan football game, concessionaires will sell an average of 65,000 bottles of water.

taking it to the streets

We've already talked about the importance of building an ambassador army and the halo effect it can have. Now, the next and potentially most important step is converting those ambassadors into walking and driving billboards. For much of what we encounter in life, seeing is believing, and your program's perception won't be changed unless people see its strength with their own eyes. Share of voice on the street (meaning how many people are wearing branded merchandise or driving cars featuring logos of your university) is critical to the perception of your program. It's up to you to ensure your voice is loudest and strongest locally, regionally, and for a select group, nationally. Do everything in your power to equip these ambassadors with the tools needed to promote your program.

"roll tide"

From July 1, 2012, to June 30, 2013, three institutions sold more licensed merchandise than any other school in the nation: the University of Texas, the University of Alabama, and Notre Dame University (Collegiate Licensing Company, August 12, 2013). As such, their voices rang the loudest, especially when it came to their respective parts of the country. One school, Alabama, didn't stop there. The Crimson Tide has taken the next step in establishing its voice on the street through its school mantra, "Roll Tide." If you haven't been to an Alabama sporting event, it's worth going, if only to walk around the tarmac of the stadium or arena and hear all of the "Roll Tides" fans throw at one another. Alabama has created a familial bond among its fans through these two simple words, much like the bond motorcyclists have built through their two-finger salute as they pass each other on the road. The Roll Tide phenomenon has become so popular that ESPN decided a couple of years back to dedicate thirty seconds of precious ad space to poke fun at the ridiculous scenarios in which Alabama fans use the phrase.

Every school has fanatics; it's simply a matter of supporting and encouraging that fanaticism.

mi casa es su casa

Fans of your program will deck out their homes and offices in your school's color and insignia if you provide them with the tools. This not only furthers their loyalty to your school, it also gets the attention of their friends and family, some of whom are potential fans. Having school paraphernalia in someone's home or on display outside of the home (I'm a big fan of the house flag—great for the brand) shows passion, and people are attracted to passion. Those potential fans can quickly transition to full-fledged fans if you equip their friends, whom they trust, with the right sales tools.

put a logo on it...again

Car decals have become a popular way of displaying allegiance to a particular university. Because of that they are important tools in your branding arsenal. What makes these even more valuable is the cost; decals are cheap. Find ways to get them into the hands and on the cars of your fans. During one game each season, hand out logo decals to the first ten thousand fans who enter the stadium. Choose a less attractive game to provide added incentive and help fill the stadium while also ensuring your most loyal fans and the fans most likely to cover their cars with university insignia receive the decal. In less than twenty-four hours, you will have increased your share of voice as compared to your cross-town rival. One thing that kills me when I see universities wasting opportunities to build the perception of their programs through potential brand-building giveaways. Instead they hand out thunder sticks and pom-poms that go straight into the trash after the game or, if they do make it home, never see the light of day again.

look over here!

Car magnets, much like car flags, can also make an impression and are easy for fans to put on. Make them big, bold, and loud! Magnets on their own scream fandom, but pair them with a group of car flags, and suddenly you have yourself a fan-mobile that can't be missed on the highway.

how many flags can fit on a suburban?

Car flags are one of my favorite pieces of collateral. As a fan, I love car flags; as a brand marketer, I love them even more. I suggest giving away flags bearing your school logo at every opportunity. Driving to a game while surrounded by hundreds of car flags all flaunting your school's logo can be one of the proudest moments a fan can have. You feel part of something bigger than yourself during those moments. Once again imagine how a young adult or athlete might be affected by a similar experience. It's a beautiful scene, and it makes an impression.

growing tails

Some schools have more opportunity to get creative than others with their accessories, whether it be through their mascots or their stories. One example is the beaver tails that can be seen attached to the backs of automobiles of proud Oregon State University supporters. These faux beaver tails may sound tacky, but they make an impact. Off-the-wall items like beaver tails are fantastic ways of drawing attention and affecting perception, more so than magnets or flags, for two reasons: 1) they're disruptive and stand out, and 2) your initial reaction as a passerby is to think that Oregon State fans must be crazy (emphasis on crazy) about their university to put something that ridiculous on their cars.

Remember, passion pulls like a magnet. It's tactics like beaver tails that grow a fan base and put your school on the top of minds locally, regionally, and, if you create something PR worthy, nationally. Figure out a unique piece for your university and get it into the hands of your most passionate fans (i.e., the die-hard fans who attend your team's scrimmages, recruiting dinners, banquets, etc.). These are the fans who will grow a tail for you.

beaver friday

I started writing this book right after college, inspired by the love I have for my university and my utter frustration in its lack of brand awareness at the time. It was then that I went on one of the school's more popular message boards, a personal favorite of mine, stepped onto my soapbox, and delivered what I considered to be a pretty epic, Jerry Maguire–like call to arms. I was twenty-three…and slightly naïve.

In that cry for help, I proposed a slew of high-level strategies to turn the athletic department's brand around, along with microlevel tactics that would bring those strategies to life. One of the tactics was what I called Beaver Friday, a day on which all Beaver fans would wear their letters, raise their flags, and transform their Hondas into logo-covered mobile billboards. It was the tail-end of football season at the time, and I had Saturday caravans on the brain. I chose Friday for that exact reason. The easiest way to stand apart from a crowd is to literally move away from the pack and into your own wide-open space. During football season, Saturday is the day everyone puts flags up and replica jerseys on. It's crowded. That's the case in just about every state, which means the idea of fans wearing gear on Saturday is expected, and that expectation leads to white noise—white noise in which schools become lost among a sea of other like-minded universities.

I thought, *What if the same number of OSU fans who wore their gear on Saturdays wore their letters on Fridays instead? What if we branded it* Beaver Friday *to make it stick and gave fans something to rally around?* People would take notice. OSU would be the primary school represented on the streets of Oregon each Friday. If the competition was focused on Saturday, we'd pick another day and own it. If all people saw on Fridays in Oregon was OSU orange, perceptions regarding the school's popularity would start to change for the better.

From that one post, and by my consistently ringing the bell each week on the message board, people started to rally behind the idea. The concept caught on to a point where one fan actually asked the Oregon State athletic director about Beaver Friday during a formal press conference. It was starting to stick. If an idea like this, born from a single message board post by a wide-eyed twenty-three-year-old, can succeed, imagine what your team of professionals can come up with and accomplish. Just remember: sometimes, you have to zig while your competition zags.

sometimes, you have to zig while your competition zags.

vote for our school

Spirit signs might be the most basic tactic I write about in this book and potentially the one with the biggest return on investment (ROI). When I say *spirit signs*, I'm talking about the simple cardboard signs that are slightly larger than a standard piece of notebook paper and are usually passed out just before major sports seasons. They say things like, "Go Blue," or "Go Bulldogs." These are cost-effective branding tools that create an additional point of contact among fans, potential fans, recruits, and your university. Print as many as you can afford, or better yet, enlist a sponsor to help you pay for printing in exchange for its logo being placed somewhere on the sign. Pass them out to your fans at games and send them to your alumni, along with a number on the back that people can call to order more for their friends and family. Encourage your community to put these in their home windows just as they would do to signify their loyalty to a potential presidential candidate during campaign season. Imagine one of your coaches driving a high school athlete around town during

"little things": when executed on a large scale, they're not little anymore.

a recruiting visit, and in every window that athlete sees a sign supporting your university. How do you think that kid is going to feel about your school and community? College towns are attractive. It's the little tactics like these that can go a long way in creating the college-town atmosphere recruits and parents love. Remember this about the "little things": when executed on a large scale, they're not little anymore.

unpaid historians

If your program has a history worth talking about, talk about it! Provide your fan base with videos or literature about your program. If you don't tell people how great your program is, how will they find out? History is something that can never be changed, and if your program has had success in the past, it is important to ensure your fans know about it. This is a great way to arm your ambassadors, providing them with more tools in their efforts to recruit new members to your side. Trust me, as one of these ambassadors myself, I know these men and women are constantly looking to convert their friends and families.

The iTunes Store sells classic college football and basketball games, as well as documentaries on major college programs, while Netflix carries similar content on a subscription basis. These are great avenues to reach current and potential fans, not to mention recruits. Imagine being able to drive a potential recruit onto iTunes to download one of your program's signature victories for just a couple of dollars. Having something like that on a young man's or woman's iPhone or home computer, while he or she decides where to spend the next four to five years, can be very impactful. Guess what these recruits are watching on the return trip home?

what's in your basement?

Another mistake I often see is universities disposing of memorabilia from games or moments of the past. Whether you chronicle it or not, *never* throw old memorabilia away. There are plenty of fans out there who will put what may look like junk to good use. Reward your most loyal fans, and you will get much more in return. Find your fanatics and give them the memorabilia you were thinking about throwing out.

One specific opportunity to turn trash to treasure centers around those specific brand ambassadors who have gone so far as to create the fan-mobiles referenced earlier. You know the people I'm talking about—the ones who take an old van and paint the entire thing in your school color, cover it with memorabilia, change the horn to your fight song, and by doing so become something of a local legend. Those are the fans who make college sports so great, and it's those fans who will bring in new blood. They'll put your memorabilia to use, as I said, but they'll also make sure it gets seen.

it's about timing

Before we part ways and you go off to build the next great college sports dynasty, I want to talk timing. It can make or break a brand moment or a brand in general.

There is a very brief period after success in which all eyes are on your program. At that point you have a tremendous opportunity to sway the opinions of thousands, including potential fans, students, recruits, and parents of potential recruits. Strike while the iron is hot, and from there turn up the heat. Timing is of the essence. As Seth Godin says in his writings and speeches, "If you wait until there is another case study in your industry, you will be too late." This window to react is closely related to the media and what they consider newsworthy. The media dictate our society's opinion on what's important, why it's important, and for how long it will be important. With that, there are two windows of opportunity in which it's imperative to take advantage of your success.

big window

Football provides an interesting example of how short your window of opportunity is after a successful season. Let's create a hypothetical situation using your university, a situation similar to the one I lived through as a senior brand and digital manager at adidas when Notre Dame advanced to the BCS National Championship in 2012. Say your university is fortunate enough to make it to the BCS National Championship game just as the Irish did. It's an incredible accomplishment, but not one you can wait to capitalize on or promote.

You have two windows in this instance, each with very different life spans. The first window is *before* the game itself actually takes place. The regular season ends in early December; at that same time, BCS Bowls and the

National Championship matchups are announced. The actual championship takes place during the first two weeks of January, which means there is a roughly four-week window in which the spotlight is on your school. If you've ever watched ESPN's *SportsCenter* leading up to the national championship, you know in those four weeks the conversation is centered around the championship game, with a smattering of coverage for other bowls. *This* is your window. *This* is the moment you need to turn up the heat.

Fans, recruits, parents, and media who would normally have little interest in your team are now paying close attention. Through this attention you have the opportunity to influence these individuals whom you wouldn't have had the chance to influence prior. And we're talking about a mass audience. According to Nielsen, ESPN's telecast of the 2014 Vizio BCS National Championship between Auburn and Florida State had over 25 million viewers and generated 4.4 million tweets by 1.2 million unique authors, surpassing 2013's BCS game by almost four hundred thousand tweets. (Nielsen, February 4, 2014)

25M | 4.4M | 1.2M
VIEWERS | TWEETS | UNIQUE AUTHORS

No longer are you simply speaking to a regional or even local audience— you're talking to a nation. Better yet, you have *four weeks* to do it! This window between the end of the season and the title game is a permission window, in which mass audiences give you permission to talk to them about your school. The media tell them it's okay. The media make you relevant by talking about your program, and that in turn makes you intriguing to an entire country, not just your current fans.

18.6M

ROSE BOWL
STANFORD VS
MICHIGAN ST.
ESPN

25.6M

BCS CHAMPIONSHIP
FLORIDA ST. VS
AUBURN
ESPN

16.3M

SUGAR BOWL
OKLAHOMA
VS ALABAMA
ESPN

11.4M

ORANGE BOWL
CLEMSON VS
OHIO ST.
ESPN

8.7M

CHICK-FIL-A BOWL
DUKE VS TEXAS
A&M ESPN

11.3M

FIESTA BOWL
UCF VS BAYLOR
ESPN

31
DEC 2013

1
JAN 2014

2

3

6

1.4M
TWEETS

4.4M
TWEETS

small window

The second window is *after* the game. Again we delve into the world of hypotheticals. Let's imagine for a minute your team has won the national championship (hairs rising yet?). Believe it or not, your window to talk about your school, despite now having what might sound like a much sexier story, is a fraction of what it was prior to the game. That's because the media move on quickly. The game story is over the next day. The national championship usually runs the week prior to the first weekend of the NFL Playoffs. Once the national championship game is over, the media move on to the NFL, and with them, so does the rest of the nation. Your window after the national championship is about twenty-four hours at most. And really, your best shot is to have something ready to go as soon as the clock strikes 00:00.

Now, you might say, "Our fans wouldn't move on that quickly," and I would agree with you. Your window to talk to existing fans is larger; quite honestly, they're listening all year at some level. But the problem with that thinking is that those individuals are already your fans. The fact that you won the championship does more to keep them loyal than any marketing. It's the new and potential fans we're concerned with. The idea of capitalizing on successful seasons is about bringing in new fans and growing your fan base. In 2013, the University of Michigan men's basketball program made a spectacular run to the national championship game against the University of Louisville. Its success on the court translated to success in social media, as the program owned the most-liked NCAA men's basketball Facebook page during the tournament. With that engagement, the global UM Facebook page reeled in over ten thousand new likes from the start of the tournament, while the Wolverine basketball Twitter following grew by 45 percent, garnering over 138,000 retweets (Rudgers, April 22, 2013).

You might also ask, "What if we're not in the national championship game?" or "What if we're not a football or basketball program?" The philosophy doesn't change. The windows are the same—prior to the game or match is crucial; after the event, assuming a win, is also important, but it's a much smaller window to activate.

The last point I want to make is around what happens if your team loses. Imagine you did not activate prior to the game and your team lost. You're left with nothing. No one remembers who came in second. Not only have you lost the game, you've lost any chance of increasing the size of your fan base, because you waited for what is a variable you can't control as a brand manager: on-field performance.

You have two very important windows. Plan for both, and do not miss out on pregame.

Take this same approach when planning for things like National Player of the Year candidates, the Final Four, the Frozen Four, or if you are building a baseball program, the College World Series in Omaha. It's crucial to preplan for any potential point of success that comes with a built-in hype window.

keep your glass slipper

The key during the season is to be prepared for anything, but it's especially important to be prepared for the best of circumstances. The bigger the underdog, the louder the bark after a win. If you think your team has no chance to win next week's game, that means you need to be spending that much more time preparing to react if it does, because if you don't believe it, chances are no one locally, regionally, or nationally believes it either. And that's not a bad thing.

The more unexpected the event, the more eyeballs and chatter that will be focused around your program postgame. Who would have thought Boise State was going to beat Oklahoma in the 2007 Fiesta Bowl? Who saw George Mason making it to the Final Four in 2006? No one expected either, and because of that everyone was talking about each event when it happened. Both upsets sparked national conversation among fans, media, and you better believe potential recruits. Boise State and George Mason quickly became household names nationally. Being an underdog can be a blessing in disguise—as long as you're ready to capitalize after the unimaginable happens.

What happens after a milestone victory? Your current fans become flag-waving brand ambassadors screaming from the mountaintops; your fringe fans suddenly become solid fans who have "always been there"; and most important, the media become eager to tell your story. It's as if your apple pie just won the blue ribbon, and everyone wants a piece. What happens if you don't have any pie when they get there? They move on to the next pie. People have short attention spans; you have to be ready to act.

Have digital content set to release as soon as the game ends, but don't stop there. Make a splash through advertising. Take out an ad in a national paper, run a television spot in prime time, put up a billboard in your closest major metropolis, buy the YouTube home page for a day. Do something that makes those already interested individuals say, "Wow, did you see what they did?" If you want fans to take you seriously, sometimes that means taking yourself more seriously and showing some bravado after a win. If you appear surprised by the win, not ready to react, fans will see the win as an anomaly. On the flip side, if you're ready to react and do so in a big way, showing confidence and that you expected to win, people will start taking you more seriously. It's that game of perception again. Be ready.

j-curve

One of the most personally valuable philosophies I've carried with me throughout my career is something called the J-curve. It's a visual launch strategy that extends the time in which companies have to talk about and build hype around their new releases. In the case of NCAA athletics, such releases could include things like uniform launches, facility grand openings, coaching hires, and schedules—anything your program deems newsworthy to both fans and media.

The thinking is simple: rather than waiting for launch day to begin communication, break your outreach into three segments:

announce

Work back from your launch day and pick a moment to unveil your story to the media.

sustain

Before landing on an announcement date, consider the window between your announcement and your launch. Make sure you have ample content, assets, and stories to carry the conversation for that extended period of time.

launch

Launch day is when your communication frequency and scale should peak. The first two weeks of your launch determine how successful you are. The stronger the first two weeks are, the longer your buzz, sales, and conversation "tail" will ultimately extend.

There are several benefits to the J-curve that have proven successful for me over my career. First, by breaking apart your announcement and launch, you immediately double your media coverage potential, going from one story to two. Take advantage of every opportunity you have to separate your stories into several individual moments. Second, an early announcement gives you time to drive awareness and conversation around your story. Third, the J-curve approach gives you time to educate users on what makes the forthcoming launch so special, in turn driving demand for your program prerelease. Fourth, in the case of uniforms and ticket sales, with demand comes the opportunity to push preorders, maximizing your day-one sales. Strong day-one sales can lead to a strong first two weeks, setting the tone for the longevity of your campaign.

carmouflage

During the final week of November 2013, we worked on launching one of the most disruptive pieces of equipment to ever hit a football field. It was a specially designed version of our newest adizero Football cleat covered in a zigzag pattern meant to emulate the camouflaging design car manufacturers use to disguise their latest concept cars before they are revealed. We called the pattern carmouflage.

The cleat was bold. It was brave. And it was very loud. We knew we had something polarizing on our hands, and we loved it. The only question was, how would we launch it? We needed a platform and a culture moment. Culture moments are moments or events in which a large percentage of the population is watching. They are invaluable, because they do not require you to bring the audience, which takes tremendous effort and resources. The eyes are already there, waiting for you to make a statement. Things like the Grammys in music, the presidential inauguration in politics, and the Super Bowl in football are culture moments.

The platform was college football, specifically our partner Texas A&M. The Aggies had a tremendous amount going for them. Not only were they a top-twenty team, they were also led by two of the most visible personalities in their respective positions: Quarterback Johnny Manziel and Head Coach Kevin Sumlin. Manziel was the reigning Heisman trophy winner and a fire starter when it came to media attention. Sumlin was in the midst of rampant rumors that he was the top candidate for the vacant (at the time) USC head coaching job. Anything these two touched turned into PR gold. Knowing this, and seeing the benefits of the potential exposure, A&M was quick to volunteer its program. And with that we had our platform. Now we needed a culture moment.

Before pitching the opportunity to any school, we laid out specific criteria for how this would come to life. Adizero is a key franchise for adidas Football, and it was crucial that this activation lift the perception of the brand. The criteria became:

perception	visual impact	exposure
⬇	⬇	⬇
to be worn by a top-ranked adidas program	to be worn by the entire team	to be unveiled on field during a nationally tele-vised game

Texas A&M fit each criteria perfectly and happened to be one of the sexiest teams in the country, thanks to Manziel and Sumlin.

On November 30, 2013, we had our culture moment. That night, in prime time and under the lights, the Aggies would take on the #5-ranked Missouri Tigers, who were playing for a chance to advance to the SEC title game and potentially the National Championship. There was a lot on the line.

But for me the game itself wasn't enough. Knowing how rabid the Aggie fan base is and experiencing firsthand the buzz around that matchup, we couldn't miss the opportunity to build hype prior to the launch.

One thing I learned during my time as a brand marketer in the video game industry is that when you have a rabid fan base that is dying for content and news, you have the opportunity to extend your stories well beyond their launches. I brought that philosophy with me to adidas, and we've since used it regularly to generate buzz, conversation, and hype around our NCAA programs and product launches.

In this case that approach took the form of a tease phase that executed well beyond my own expectations. Beginning on the Monday prior to the game, adidas Football and Texas A&M began socially disseminating vague imagery of the carmouflage pattern with copy laid over the top that simply read: *11.30.13.* Clearly that signaled that something was happening on that day. Media and fans alike immediately took the bait. From one single post, we had national media reporting on and posting our imagery, asking questions like, "What does Texas A&M have in store for 11.30.13?" and, "What is this pattern?"

But that was just the beginning of our plan. We had a meticulous rollout schedule during our tease phase. We knew what content would launch on which day and at what time, to the minute—all of which was coordinated with and agreed to up front by the school. We were ready to start a media frenzy.

Following another mysterious visual of the pattern, this time with an A&M logo in place of the date (though the date was always part of the communication in some way, by way of the image or post copy), we began to give people the impression that this carmouflage pattern was taking over the Aggie campus and football program.

During the time we were planning our rollout, Coach Sumlin had sparked a great deal of buzz of his own at surrounding Texas high schools (and through the media) by taking a helicopter to recruiting visits. So much so that the helicopter was given its own nickname—swagcopter—because of how much swagger it took to land a chopper at the 50-yard line of a high school football field during a visit. Coach Sumlin and his swagcopter became a national story. We had a hook at the end of our fishing line; we just needed to put a little bait on it.

Following the release of our consecutive pattern-driven visuals, we began to reveal images of iconic symbols on or around the A&M campus that had a not-so-subtle twist. The swagcopter was the first image we released. What made the image unique was that the normally subdued helicopter was now wrapped entirely in the black-and-white carmouflage pattern that people had seen in our previous posts.

Media and fans ate it up. Not only did it look great, with what looked like a new paint job (we didn't actually paint it; the pattern was applied digitally onto an existing photo), but it was another clue that something was happening around this pattern. People were begging for answers. By this time all of the major networks and blogs had written about it. Every clue that we dropped would be followed by a new media hit online. We then took over both adidas's and Texas A&M's digital channels, covering every page we could in carmouflage skin. By the time A&M released a photo of the team boarding a carmouflage-wrapped plane heading to Missouri, fans and media were dying to know what was going on.

We were finally ready to tell them. Just prior to kickoff of that Saturday night, we unveiled official imagery of our newest cleat. By doing so, when the game started, all eyes were on the Aggie players' feet. The response was tremendous. In my years working in brand marketing, I have never seen such an overwhelmingly positive reaction across the board from a specific target market. Every high school male who tweeted about the shoe was gushing over the design, A&M fan or otherwise.

Major credit goes to the design and product teams for designing a cleat that was disruptive enough to allow for such storytelling. But just as important, kudos to Texas A&M for taking a chance. There is no doubt in my mind that this activation, and activations like it that follow the J-curve, positively affect recruiting and contribute to a school's brand story. In February of 2014, three months after our carmouflage launch, Texas A&M signed the #6 overall recruiting class in the country, according to Rivals.com.

CONSISTENCY &FREQUENCY

ARE THE KEYS TO MAKING YOUR STORY STICK.
YOU CAN'T HAVE ONE WITHOUT THE OTHER.

PICK A
LOGO.

PICK A
COLOR.

EVERYTHING STARTS WITH YOUR VISUAL IDENTITY.
FOCUS ON ONE LOGO, FOCUS ON ONE COLOR, AND

◆ GO. ◆
DON'T WAIT FOR STORIES
TO COME TO YOU.

JEREMY DARLOW

CREATE YOUR OWN PR.

PAINT YOUR CHEST AND SIT IN THE STUDENT SECTION LIKE COACH PEARL.

ADD SLEEVES TO YOUR BASKETBALL JERSEYS LIKE ADIDAS.

ERECT A BILLBOARD IN NEW YORK CITY TOUTING YOUR HEISMAN TROPHY CANDIDATE LIKE THE OREGON DUCKS.

▄▄▄▄ AND THEN ▄▄▄▄

SPREAD THE WORD!

THROUGH ALUMNI
KEEP YOUR ALUMNI INVOLVED; LEVERAGE THEIR REACH TO TELL YOUR STORY.

THROUGH SOCIAL
TREAT EACH SOCIAL SPACE DIFFERENTLY. UTILIZE EACH PLATFORM'S CORE COMPETENCY TO TELL YOUR STORY.

THROUGH PAID MEDIA
DISRUPT IN KEY SPACES; USE EACH CANVAS TO TELL COMPELLING VISUAL STORIES.

YOU HAVE TWO WINDOWS AVAILABLE TO **CAPITALIZE ON SUCCESS.** DON'T MISS EITHER.

BIG WINDOW
THE FIRST WINDOW IS BEFORE YOUR KEY MOMENT TAKES PLACE, WHEN ALL EYES AND CONVERSATION ARE ON YOUR PROGRAM FOR AN EXTENDED PERIOD.

THE SECOND WINDOW COMES AFTER A KEY MOMENT AND WIN. YOU HAVE MUCH LESS TIME TO CAPITALIZE ON THIS WINDOW, SO BE PREPARED. **SMALL WINDOW**

DID I SAY CONSISTENCY AND FREQUENCY?

CH**3** HOMEWORK

✦ What do your logo and uniforms say about your program? What do you want them to say?

....

✦ How many colors do your fans wear? What color do you want them to wear?

....

✦ Count the number of logos you see on a daily basis for every school in your area. Which school has the biggest share of voice in your town?

....

✦ What makes your in-game experience unique? What does it say about your program? How can you improve? Are you telling a story?

....

◆ For what key moments in the next three to five years do you anticipate
needing to be ready? Are you ready?

....

◆ What matters most when it comes to making your story stick? (Hint:
there's a right answer.)

....

notes

....

conclusion
first and ten, do it again

Each of these tactics can be effective in your quest to create a long-term relationship among potential fans, recruits, and your university. However, success lies in the frequency and consistency of your message. Imagine the effect on perception that multiple points of branding contact can have on an individual who has yet to form allegiance to one school or another.

Think about your efforts to tell your story this way: in a typical morning, a potential recruit may come across two or three people wearing your school's apparel (someone in a T-shirt here, another in a hat there), while later in that same day, on the way to lunch, he may see a flag with your university's logo on it waving from one car and a prominent decal featured on another. While driving through a neighborhood that night, he may spot a house with a sign in the window in your school's color and with your mascot and motto on it. His destination that night may actually be to the home of an alum or current fan of your school, who happens to have a nice collection of sports memorabilia from your program that she likes to show off. All told, that's around six points of contact with your program's brand in one day. That young man will go to sleep fully aware of the passion and strength of your program, and it's that passion and strength that draw in new fans and land blue-chip recruits. Consistency. Frequency.

As I finished writing this book, I found myself in the middle of a brand-positioning exercise for one of adidas's top NCAA properties, bouncing between my work on the program and finishing up the last bits of writing. It was then that I realized just how lucky we are and how fun this process really is. That's a key point: this is fun. It's important to keep that in mind as you dig in for the long haul, because the one thing I can guarantee you with 100 percent certainty is this: it's not going to be easy. It's going to take time. It's going to consume you. But I can also guarantee you that it will be worth it.

The good news is that you're holding in your hands your guide to making the process easier. In this book we've talked about three steps to building your brand:

managing your perception

Remember that perception is reality, and smoke and mirrors are sometimes all you need, at least to start. Rome wasn't built in a day, and neither is a sustainable national championship–level program. Find your wins and accentuate them while at the same time building around them.

writing your story

You're going to want to skip the big dig or at the very least cut it short. It's an exhausting task, but fight that urge. The more diligent you are up front, the more successful and defensible your brand story is from that point on.

telling your story

Two words: *consistency* and *frequency*, in case you forgot. Find your voice and own it. The more consistent you are, the more likely it is to stick. From there, it's all about getting your message in front of your audience as many times and in as many different places as possible.

It might sound crazy, but that's all you need. When it comes down to it, successful marketing plans and brands are built from a few key pillar strategies. Accomplish these three steps and you will have a stronger brand than you had before you started. I truly believe that. I've seen it happen.

We're all looking for the same thing: the championship. Build your brand; wear the crown. You have the roadmap; now it's up to you to take your brand to the promised land.

recommended reading

Bedbury, Scott
✦ *A New Brand World: Eight Principles for Achieving Brand Leadership in the 21st Century*
New York: Viking Penguin, 2002.

Dosh, Kristi
✦ *Saturday Millionaires: How Winning Football Builds Winning Colleges*
New York: Turner Publishing Company, 2013.

Godin, Seth
✦ *All Marketers Are Liars: The Power of Telling Authentic Stories in a Low-Trust World*
New York: Portfolio, 2004.
✦ *Purple Cow: Transform Your Business by Being Remarkable*
New York: Portfolio, 2003.

Kerner, Noah, and Gene Pressman
✦ *Chasing Cool: Standing Out in Today's Cultured Marketplace*
New York: Atria Books, 2007.

Li, Charlene, and Josh Bernoff
✦ *Groundswell: Winning in a World Transformed by Social Technologies*
Boston: Forrester Research, Inc., 2008.

bibliography

Bedbury, Scott
✦ *A New Brand World: Eight Principles for Achieving Brand Leadership in the 21st Century.* New York: Viking Penguin, 2002.

Cohen, Ben
✦ "R.I.P., Heisman Campaign: Traditional Publicity Blitzes for College Football's Premier Award are Dying." *Wall Street Journal*, August 20, 2013. http://online.wsj.com/news/articles/SB10001424127887323423804579024624018427850.

Collegiate Licensing Company
✦ "Collegiate Licensing Company Names Top Selling Universities and Manufacturers for 2012–13." Collegiate Licensing Company website, August 22, 2013. http://www.clc.com/News/Rankings-Annual-2012-13.aspx.

Duggan, Maeve
✦ "Social Media Update 2013: 42% of Online Adults Use Multiple Social Networking Sites, But Facebook Remains the Platform of Choice." Pew Research Center, December 30, 2013. http://www.pewinternet.org/2013/12/30/social-media-update-2013.

Gesenhues, Amy
✦ "Arby's Social Media Manager Gives Inside Scoop on Tweet to Pharrell that Rocked the Grammys." Marketing Land, January 29, 2014. http://marketingland.com/guy-behind-arbys-tweet-pharrell-williams-rocked-grammys-72222.

Godin, Seth
✦ *All Marketers Are Liars: The Power of Telling Authentic Stories in a Low-Trust World.* New York: Portfolio, 2004.
✦ "What if Your Slogan Is True?" *Seth's Blog*, August 19, 2012. http://sethgodin.typepad.com/seths_blog/2012/08/what-if-your-slogan-is-true.html.

Juniper Research
✦ "Mobile Ad Spend to Approach $40 Billion Annually by 2018, Finds Juniper Research." Juniper Research, October 22, 2013. http://www.juniperresearch.com/viewpressrelease.php?pr=406.

Nielsen

♦ "Commercial Breaks Aren't Tweet Breaks." Nielsen, September 18, 2013. http://www.nielsen.com/us/en/newswire/2013/commercial-breaks-arent-tweet-breaks.html.

♦ "Year in the Sports Media Report: 2013." Nielsen, February 4, 2014. http://www.nielsen.com/us/en/insights/reports/2014/year-in-the-sports-media-report-2013.html.

♦ "That's Amore: Americans' Love Affair with Sports Extends across Screens." Nielsen, February 13, 2014. http://www.nielsen.com/us/en/newswire/2014/thats-amore-americans-love-affair-with-sports-extends-across-screens.html.

♦ "The Follow-Back: Understanding the Two-Way Causal Influence between Twitter Activity and TV Viewership." Nielsen, August 6, 2013. http://www.nielsen.com/us/en/newswire/2013/the-follow-back--understanding-the-two-way-causal-influence-betw.html.

♦ "Tops of 2013 TV and Social Media." Nielsen, December 17, 2013. http://www.nielsen.com/us/en/newswire/2013/tops-of-2013-tv-and-social-media.html.

Price, Darlene

♦ *Well Said! Presentations and Conversations that Get Results.* New York: AMACOM, 2012.

Reich, Brian, and Dan Solomon

♦ *Media Rules! Mastering Today's Technology to Connect with and Keep Your Audience.* New York: Wiley, 2007.

Richter, Felix

♦ "Consumers Still Trust Traditional Media Advertising Over Online Ads." Statisa.com, January 8, 2014. http://www.statista.com/chart/1473/consumer-trust-in-advertising.

♦ "Tablets to Outsell PCs Worldwide by 2015." Statista.com, March 1, 2014. http://www.statista.com/chart/1138/tablet-and-pc-shipment-forecast/.

Rudgers, Lisa M.

♦ "Amazing Impact." *View from the Cube*, April 22, 2013. http://vpcomm.umich.edu/lisa-rudgers/2013/04/amazing-impact.

Smallwood, Brad

♦ "Making Digital Brand Campaigns Better." Facebook Studio, October 1, 2012. https://www.facebook-studio.com/news/item/making-digital-brand-campaigns-better.

Statista

♦ "Age Breakdown of Video Game Players in the United States in 2014." Statista.com, 2014. http://www.statista.com/statistics/189582/

age-of-us-video-game-players
-since-2010/

◆"Global Video Games Revenue
from 2012 to 2015 (in Billion U.S.
Dollars)." Statista.com, 2014. http://
www.statista.com/statistics/237187/
global-video-games-revenue.

◆ "Revenue of the United States
Fast Food Restaurant Industry
from 2002 to 2018 (in Billion U.S.
Dollars)." Statista.com, 2014. http://
www.statista.com/statistics/196614/
revenue-of-the-us-fast-food-restau
rant-industry-since-2002.

◆ "Social Media Marketing Expenditure in the United States from 2011
to 2016 (in Billion U.S. Dollars)."
Statista.com, 2014. http://www.
statista.com/statistics/276890/
social-media-marketing-
expenditure-in-the-united-states.

Statistic Brain
◆ "Attention Span Statistics." Statistic Brain, 2014. http://www.statis
ticbrain.com/attention-span-statis
tics.

Texas A&M Athletics
◆ "Study: End of Football Season
Produced $37 Million in Media Ex-
posure for Texas A&M." Texas A&M
Official Athletic Site, January 18,
2013. http://www.12thman
.com/ViewArticle.dbml?AT
CLID=206020080.

Thielman, Stan
◆ "You Won't Believe How Big
TV Still Is: Staggering Viewership
Numbers and Dominant Revenue
Figures." *Adweek*, March 2, 2014.
http://www.adweek.com/news/tech
nology/you-wont-believe-how-big-
tv-still-156039.

Vint, Patrick
◆ "2013 Spring Game Attendance
Rankings: Auburn and Alabama Top
Standings." SBNation.com, April 21,
2013. http://www.sbnation.com/col
lege-football/2013/4/21/4248898/
spring-football-game-attendance-
2013-auburn.

thank you

to all of my friends who supported me along the way.
I wouldn't have been able to do it without you.

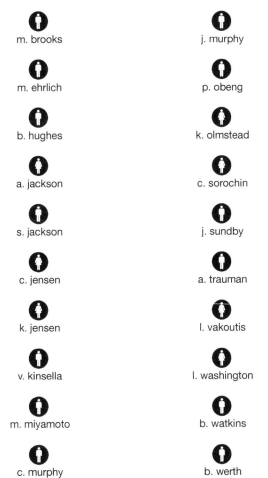

m. brooks

m. ehrlich

b. hughes

a. jackson

s. jackson

c. jensen

k. jensen

v. kinsella

m. miyamoto

c. murphy

j. murphy

p. obeng

k. olmstead

c. sorochin

j. sundby

a. trauman

l. vakoutis

l. washington

b. watkins

b. werth

Printed in the USA
CPSIA information can be obtained
at www.ICGtesting.com
LVHW060840151223
766592LV00005B/24

* 9 7 8 0 9 9 0 5 6 2 2 0 7 *